JOURNEY TO THE RIVER

*Spiritual Insight & Practical Wisdom to Help
You Endure the Inner Healing Journey*

Cheray James

A Revealing Sons Resource

Copyright © 2019. Cheray James

All Rights Reserved.

All rights reserved. No part of this book may be reproduced or transmitted in any form or by any means, electronic or mechanical, including photocopying, recording, or by an information storage and retrieval system - except by a reviewer who may quote brief passages in a review to be printed in a magazine or newspaper - without permission in writing from the publisher or author.

ISBN-13: 978-1-7333465-0-4

ISBN-10: 1-7333465-0-3

Library of Congress Control Number: 2019910198

Published By Revealing Sons, LLC

revealingsons@gmail.com

Visit Revealing Sons at revealingsons.com

For a people pursuing freedom and wholeness.

Foreword

Twenty-first century prophetic scribe, innovative, creative, out-of-the-box thinker and compassionate minister are just a few words to describe Cheray James. Many in the world may not be familiar with her name or ministry now, but they will be. God is raising up a new breed of radical sons with clarity and passionate pursuit concerning the releasing of the purposes of God and the revealing of sons. Cheray has received the burden of the Father and is answering the call through pen and the production of kingdom resources to equip believers to live in freedom and power.

The need for inner healing is more essential in these critical times than mere physical healing. Inner Healing must be ministered to the heart, mind and memories. Jesus says, "What does it profit a man to gain the whole world and forfeit his soul?" (Mark 8:36). Our souls are of great value to God. He died to save them. Your soul makes you the person you are. You can have all the money in the world, but your soul can be depressed, starved, scarred, scared and severely hurting. The thresholds of the pain of the past can be so high, they block your ability to live healed through the power of Christ. The soul can and should experience the healing power of Christ's salvation.

In *The Journey*, Cheray authentically reveals her journey of healing and restoration to release practical healing keys into the life and soul of the reader. She invites the reader to complete practical and doable applications to discover and remove barriers and blockages to living as a free soul. She introduces living examples and the living Words of Christ to wash the memory and heart of the pains of the past.

Cheray ultimately invites the precious soul to come to the waters of life and to be made whole. She skillfully reveals the truths and bumps of the journey, but also the value and freedoms of the worthy voyage.

I have had the privilege to facilitate and to witness her swim in the waters of healing. The fruit of her journey is evidenced in her message and character. I have been tremendously blessed by this fresh new apostolic engineer and recommend *The Journey* for the healing of the soul.

Dr. Kim Y. Black

JOURNEY TO THE RIVER

Preface

I extend love to you beautiful soul. I thank you for picking up this book. In fact, I am hopeful about your experience with its contents. There are many books that you could probably pick up that speak on self-help and healing. There are several schools of thought as it pertains to healing and wholeness and the methods to reach both. There are many approaches applied to gain emotional and mental health. Seemingly, there are more astute authors and professionals that have material that you could use to aid you in you inner healing process. Many of them would purport that they have the solution to all of your healing needs. As the writer of this book, I won't assert that claim. This book is not even intended to prescribe the solution for your healing process. I am wise enough to know that there is no cookie cutter approach to healing a soul. Souls are far too unique and have a myriad of complexities in their individuality for me to ever claim to have the know how for the healing of each—especially not in one text. However, there is a power that comes with identifying what this book is intended for. If you have this book, I believe that you are preparing for a journey that will encapsulate your specific healing process. This book is the precursor to that experience. (Or maybe the exhortation you need to stay on the journey you have already begun.) If you will, picture this book as a "guide for the journey". This writing is intended to breakthrough the wall of fears, uncertainties, preplanned discomforts, hindrances, and traps in order to help you immerse your soul in God's healing waters.

I know that many people, the world over are in dire need for their emotional and mental selves to be healed. If you have this book, that probably includes you. You may have lived out more years of trauma then some have seen in years of life altogether. Even knowing that fact, it is my belief and understanding that many of us don't ever attain our healing. This is not out of a lack of desire. Many of us can never make it across the various thresholds that this journey presents to us. The degrees of difficulty that come with facing the pain in our history often choke out the will to persevere until we see the intended outcome. There are so many things in our way that come to hinder and literally block us from our pursuit or the will power thereof. Often times, our own minds stage a hostile takeover to our hearts and keep us from the labor -intensive work that we need to endure for healing to take place. Life simply keeps going and we tend to make priorities out of the things that have the loudest alarms or biggest fires. I am sure that I can throw a rock in any direction and hit a thousand people that this applies to.

As confidently as I know this, I also know that God, Our Heavenly Father (I call Him *Abba*) wants us to be healed. In fact, when His Son Jesus died and was resurrected, he negotiated a covenant for us that included our total healing. If you already belong to God, you are living beneath your birthright by living with pain in your heart. Abba wants all of his children made whole. Abba's love and heart for his people made an indelible impression. He has impressed upon me just how much it pains Him to see His children hurting the way that they do. He does not just care about us being physically whole. He does not simply care about our spiritual aptitude. He understands just how he designed us. If our souls are not healthy, neither can our bodies be. He understands that the quality of our souls determines the quality of the lives that we will lead. He understands that the power we wield from our spirit has to be filtered through our soul. He understands that he gets the highest amount of glory from our lives when we are completely healed and whole people. There is no success in destiny fulfillment without dealing with our brokenness.

Abba does not look pass our souls to just see about our spirits. In fact, He has always been after our souls. After He goes about making us alive in the spirit through the salvation and rebirth experience, the rest of our journey has to do with Him renovating our souls—brick by brick—layer-by-layer—piece by piece. We live out our destiny and relate to Him through our souls. We interact with one another through the soul. All things pertaining to life flow through the soul. When the soul is not whole, neither can any of the rest of these things be. This is a big deal to Abba. He did not send Jesus to die so that we can remain broken souls living a spiritual, yet pitiful life. In fact, He is personally impacted when we aren't able to live out the fullness of all that He planned for us. He is grieved when we don't become the people He spoke and constructed us to be. It is from this point of view that this book was written.

You may be saying to yourself, "Well, He is God! Why did He allow us to experience the pain in the first place?" With that in mind, you have to understand that there are many spiritual forces that interact with us in the Earth. Free will is a double-edged sword. Honestly, people have the right to be whoever they want to be and in some instances that will have negative outcomes for other people on the planet. We are often fans of the liberty that comes with free will as so long as it does not have a negative consequence for our lives. Free will gives people the option to choose who their god is and what voices they will follow. They choose what their moral code will be. There are things that happen on this planet that are not God's desire or plan for our lives. He is not helpless but He is integral to His word and how He would govern this planet. Now, in that, He is still hurt by the things that hurt us and move us from what He desires on our behalf. This is why He is very persistent with the saving of souls. This is why He is so adamant about getting us to the place of freedom and liberty so that healing and restoration can happen. For those of us that belong to Him, He can take everything that was meant for our bad and make it work out to benefit us. He can reverse the effects of trauma. He can brings us back to our original state—before the wounds were inflicted.

Abba knows that the journey back to wholeness is not so simple or easy. He knows that healing and restoration are not walks in the park. He knows that they both can take time and happen across seasons. His initial priority is to create an opening in the fortresses we create in order to try to keep us from any more pain. We put these guards around our hearts as a defense mechanism. What we don't realize is that, we aren't just protecting ourselves from contaminated streams; we are also missing out on the clean streams of His healing waters. So Abba instructed me to give you this book to allow its contents to cut open a path that will lead you to His healing waters. He will be the one to take you through your healing. Once you are open, then, you can start healing. So I ask you to follow me on the preemptive discourse to ready you for your journey in soul healing. Through this book, let Abba get you ready for the road ahead. Let him lead you on this journey so that the waters can wash over your life. Today is the day that Abba helps you begin your JOURNEY TO THE RIVER.

TABLE OF CONTENTS

FOREWORD	III
JOURNEY TO THE RIVER	V
PREFACE	V

PART 1 JOURNEY PRINCIPLES

INTRODUCTION	1
CHAPTER 1 – NAAMAN'S JOURNEY	5
JOURNEY THOUGHTS | CHAPTER 1	24

PART 2 WISDOM ON THE WAY

CHAPTER 2 – TIME IS RELATIVE	26
JOURNEY THOUGHTS | CHAPTER 2	36
CHAPTER 3 – AVOIDING SOUL PLACEBOS	37
JOURNEY THOUGHTS | CHAPTER 3	48
CHAPTER 4 – SYMPTOMS SPEAK	49
JOURNEY THOUGHTS | CHAPTER 4	57
CHAPTER 5 – OWN YOUR PAIN	58
JOURNEY THOUGHTS | CHAPTER 5	70
CHAPTER 6 – THE POWER OF FULL DISCLOSURE	71
JOURNEY THOUGHTS | CHAPTER 6	82

PART 3 WISDOM FOR THE STAY

CHAPTER 7 – STERILE HEALING ENVIRONMENTS	85
JOURNEY THOUGHTS | CHAPTER 7	95
CHAPTER 8 – YOU CAN HEAL WRONG	96
JOURNEY THOUGHTS | CHAPTER 8	105
CHAPTER 9 – SEQUENTIAL EFFECTS OF HEALING	106
JOURNEY THOUGHTS | CHAPTER 9	115

PART 4 STRENGTH FOR YOUR JOURNEY

CHAPTER 10 – TESTIMONIES	117
CHAPTER 11 – PRAYERS FOR THE JOURNEY	131
CHAPTER 12 – FINAL WORDS OF WISDOM	141

Part 1
Journey Principles

JOURNEY TO THE RIVER

Introduction

Okay, beautiful soul! I want to be sure that you understand how to use this book so that you can get the most from its contents. As I have said, this book is not intended to be the end all for your personal healing. It is a wisdom-filled consult to help you get prepared for many of things that will come next. The effort in these pages is intended to remove as many things as possible that will keep you blocked in and hindered from taking your journey to the healing waters. This book is constructed with very practical wisdom in mind. Imagine yourself having a conversation with a relative in your family who has gone through this journey ahead of you.

This book is constructed to convey very practical wisdom and simple spiritual principles. This book is designed to allow you to hear the heart of Abba as it pertains to the value that He assigns to your wholeness. Much of this book's contents were gathered from a stream of communication with the Holy Spirit over the course of a couple of weeks. He would point out very specific and natural examples found in my life (and most likely yours) to convey a truth that is needed in order to heal the way Abba intends for us to.

This book starts off with a biblical story of a man named Naaman. Abba uses him as a case study and a prophetic picture of how he looks at all of us who need to be healed. In the first chapter we deeply explore the spiritual principles that can be extracted from Naaman's life. If you listen carefully, you will hear what Abba is saying to your heart through Naaman's life. You will begin to understand some of the current and coming events in your life as you set out to take your journey.

Naaman's journey culminates with him being completely healed by immersing in the Jordan River. Like Naaman, we will all have a *river*. The river is the designated place where the spirit of God is in operation and synchronized with our yielded hearts. Each person's *river* will be different. The particulars of the *river* encounter will be different. However, we all have to take the *Journey to the River*. The following eight chapters are intended to convey wisdom for each stage. Rather you are preparing to go, already en route, or actually about to get in the water—there is wisdom here for you.

In those eight chapters are a combination of precautions, potential outcomes, and preparatory caveats that will aid preemptively as you make your way to the river. It is Abba's heart that you be as prepared as possible for the journey ahead. Most people can endure the process of healing if they are mentally and emotionally prepared for what is coming. People tend to quit prematurely when they are taken by surprise. Some choose not to remain on the *surgery table* when things are done unexpectedly. Abba wants our full cooperation on this journey of healing. It really takes a partnership between Him and us to get to the fully desired outcome. We have to be willing participants. We have to learn what we need and what we should and should not be doing before, during and after the process like any good patient. We have to make commitments to follow the *doctor's* orders. The book is intended to flow like that.

At the end of each of the first nine chapters, there are pages called *Journey Thoughts*. These pages contain questions that correspond to the chapters to help connect the wisdom to your life. They are meant to provoke thought and spark internal dialogue as you prepare to take your journey.

The final section of this book is solely dedicated to strengthen your heart and mind for all of the things you will face or that face you on this journey. It is my attempt at propelling you toward the waters by the time you reach this books end. This section is three chapters that include prayers, testimonies, and final words of wisdom. The testimonies are meant to be a source of encouragement. They are river journey stories of brother and sisters who may be just like you. They share how God interrupted their lives to draw them to His waters. They also share how the *river* changed their lives for the best. You can draw strength from those who have gone through this process before you. The prayers are intended to support you and energize you when you are feeling like you want to quit. These prayers are meant to speak to your spirit to edify you while you are being restored. And the final words of wisdom are my parting gift as you set out on your journey to the river.

The goal is that, by the time you take in the wisdom from this book, you will be completely ready for your journey of inner healing. You will be ready for Abba to take you into the depths of His healing waters. It is my hope that the wisdom from these pages will be echoes in your heart while you cross the various thresholds. I imagine that these words would stay with you and cling to your heart and fuel you to make it through to the end. Read these pages, as many times you need to. Let your heart be deeply informed and fully persuaded by wisdom's voice. Hear her speak deeply into your heart.

JOURNEY TO THE RIVER

Chapter 1 – Naaman's Journey

STARTING HERE

Peace be unto you, dear friend. There is an impending healing journey upon you. Although it may be uncomfortable, it is surely worth it. I had been listening and leaning into a conversation with Abba for a couple of weeks and He had such intense and invested interest in your ability to start your healing journey. I want to start you at the top of the conversation where He started with me about healing. One night while working, I was listening to scripture in my hearing while executing my job task. I had actually started out listening for a specific scripture but I let the book keep playing. By the time I had really focused back in, I begin to hear the story of Naaman playing in my ear. As I listened to his story, Abba started blowing up the wisdom of Naaman's life in my heart. It was almost like He was decoding the story as it was playing. I believe that Naaman's life is a prophetic picture and forecast to many of our stories and journeys in the healing process. Let us use his story as a case study to extract the wisdom of God from.

NAAMAN'S JOURNEY

I do not want to assume that you heard Naaman's story before. Let us revisit his story how the bible tells it specifically.

Naaman, commander of the army of the king of Syria, was a great man with his master and in high favor, because by him the Lord had given victory to Syria. He was a mighty man of valor, but he was a leper. Now the Syrians on one of their raids had carried off a little girl from the land of Israel, and she worked in the service of Naaman's wife. She said to her mistress, "Would that my lord were with the prophet who is in Samaria! He would cure him of his leprosy." So Naaman went in and told his lord, "Thus and so spoke the girl from the land of Israel." And the king of Syria said, "Go now, and I will send a letter to the king of Israel."

So he went, taking with him ten talents of silver, six thousand shekels of gold, and ten changes of clothing. And he brought the letter to the king of Israel, which read, "When this letter reaches you, know that I have sent to you Naaman my servant, that you may cure him of his leprosy." And when the king of Israel read the letter, he tore his clothes and said, "Am I God, to kill and to make alive, that this man sends word to me to cure a man of his leprosy? Only consider, and see how he is seeking a quarrel with me."

But when Elisha the man of God heard that the king of Israel had torn his clothes, he sent to the king, saying, "Why have you torn your clothes? Let him come now to me, that he may know that there is a prophet in Israel."

So Naaman came with his horses and chariots and stood at the door of Elisha's house. And Elisha sent a messenger to him, saying, "Go and wash in the Jordan seven times, and your flesh shall be restored, and you shall be clean." But Naaman was angry and went away, saying, "Behold, I thought that he would surely come out to me and stand and call upon the name of the Lord his God, and wave his hand over the place and cure the leper. Are not Abana and Pharpar, the rivers of Damascus, better than all the waters of Israel? Could I not wash in them and be clean?" So he turned and went away in a rage. But his servants came near and said to him, "My father, it is a great word the prophet has spoken to you; will you not do it? Has he actually said to you, 'Wash, and be clean'?" So he went down and dipped himself seven times in the Jordan, according to the word of the man of God, and his flesh was restored like the flesh of a little child, and he was clean. **2 Kings 5:1-14**

There is so much insight to unpack from this story—from this journey. Naaman's life can be a picture of any of us and if you discern the wisdom of his life story, you will make it to your *river* and be healed also. Let us look at the spiritual insight extracted from His Journey.

SUCCESS CANNOT HIDE PAIN

The very first thing that we can extract from Naaman's journey is that success does not hide pain. His story starts off giving us great details about how accomplished he was. He was a great army commander.

God used him to lead his nation to victory. He had great favor with the king of his nation. It even notes that he was a mighty man of valor or a person of great courage. However, all of these things listed and culminated with a hard truth—he was a leper. All of his status and accomplishments did nothing to conceal his pain. No matter the accolades that he attained over his military career, his condition remained. He was a man of great leadership abilities, but that did not take away his need for healing.

Many of us, just like Naaman, are well accomplished in our fields of study and/or professional careers. We have amassed wealth and status or live manageable lives. We become people of great reputation and some of us have connections with the upper echelon of our industries and realms of influence. However, the one thing that causes us the greatest pain is still glaringly obvious. It is not as hidden as we hoped it would be with all that we have done. We have not been able to out-run the pains of our history. We often believe that success in our professional careers and public lives will create a barrier between our unaddressed pain and us. That could not be further from the truth. Many times the pain becomes even more obvious.

It would seem that if you had a lot of success and accomplishments, you would be happier. It would seem that you would be most satisfied with your life. It would seem that you would have a handle on your self. The world would assume you to have the most joy and brightest spirit in the room. The reality is that many of you feel alone because of your pain. You feel the heaviest. You are the one in a room full of light but only able to see the darkness. You are the one dealing with depression. Why? Because, success cannot hide your pain. Success (on any level) does nothing for the things that hurt you. In fact, material possessions and public success that you amass only magnify the real you. Whoever you are is massively blown up when you get access to things you didn't have before. You become more of that person. You also become more aware of the real condition of your soul.

A great deal of the millennial generation has hit this ceiling. Many of us did well or are progressively doing well as professionals and entrepreneurs. We let our pains push us and fuel our ambitions for success. Many believed that success would be the best revenge for those that hurt us. It was believed that it would be the greatest smack in the face for those that abandoned and neglected us. We believed that it would shutdown *our* haters. What no one told our generation is that pain does not just leave. The scary truth is that pain will embed itself into the personality of the soul it inhabits until it is intercepted by a greater power. Many people (in general) are makeshift versions of themselves because of the pain buried inside of them.

I often hear "that's just how I am" as a blanket statement to excuse the broken nature and negative behaviors of a soul that has done nothing to address its pain. Many people believe that they are genuinely callus, angry, short-tempered, withdrawn, and despondent or any number of things. This is because they have never witnessed themselves in a state of true wholeness. They don't realize that this personality trait is an adaptation or mutation that has happened to accommodate the weight of the pain in their hearts. Success cannot do anything to conceal this. The degrees, the bank account, the material possessions, the passport stamps, the business deals, the likes and follows on social media, and all will be great items on the list of noteworthy things about your life. But just like Namaan, the list will culminate with and be overshadowed by this one statement—but he (or she) was a leper.

Now, of course leprosy is an actual physical disease and so I do not mean for that to be taken literally. Leprosy is a disease caused by slow growing bacteria that eventually attacks the nervous system and respiratory system, cause muscle weakness, and the development of skin sores. Just like leprosy, childhood pains can be like slow growing bacteria. Left unattended, it will impact your most important systems of functioning. It starts internally and then eventually becomes apparent to everyone around you. It can leave you emotionally and mentally crippled or even paralyzed.

Another important thing to note is that, the story does not tell us how Naaman got the leprosy. Naturally, we know that leprosy can be contracted from another person that shares close quarters with us. At some point he was possibly vulnerable or exposed to someone that caused him to get it. In the bible, people were also stricken with leprosy as a consequence to a bad choice.

These two hypothetical possibilities are important to consider because they let us know that the origin of your pain is not as significant to God as your need to be healed. Many of us disqualify ourselves from healing because of the origin and/ or source but God does not.

Overall, it is important that you understand no matter the success, you are still at risk and need to address your pain. It is Abba's desire to help you become really successful from the inside out.

UNUSUAL SOURCES

As we move forward in the story, we are able to extract another principle from Naaman's life. It seems like the highlight of Naaman's condition came out of left field. You will find that God may begin to put the light on your pain at the most inconvenient or irrelevant time. It seems like at the height of all of Naaman's success, he begin to feel the weight of his pain. You may find that you are already there or very close to that place. You will find that an intense amount of pressure starts to show up to identify your problem areas in the midst of some of your highest highs. This pressure will create an atmosphere fit for wisdom and direction to find you. Now, what you will have to address in order to receive it is your arrogance, pride, and ego. God may begin to put wisdom in the mouth of people and places that you are not used to receiving from. In some cases they may have a lower status than you. They may not be as accomplished as you are. They may not be in your tax bracket. They may not be at your rank. They may not be an integral part of your *circle*. They may have a very arbitrary reason to share your space, but in that moment you must be able to be sensitive.

The story says that Naaman went to his own house and there was servant girl there who was carried off from Israel through war. She was a servant to his wife. However, in this scenario, she was the one giving the wisdom to point Naaman to the place and person that would bring him healing. You see, Naaman had to lay all of his accomplishments and status to the side and hear the wisdom in the mouth of someone who was a servant to him. Can you discern the wisdom of God without being dismissively judgmental about the person it comes from? God will place the wisdom for your impending journey in unusual sources. He may direct you to unassuming places and to unknown people. It is His power that does the healing no matter the instrument or facilitators used. He has the right to direct you as He wills. It is your responsibility to hear and respond. Naaman was able to hear the wisdom of the young servant girl and he responded to it. We know that because the next recorded action was Naaman going to tell his King what she said. This is the time that you must hear wisdom—no matter how unusual the source—and respond to it.

HEALING HAS COSTS

Naaman's story continues to be filled with principles that can aid us in our lives, as we would move on the journey toward healing. The story continues to say that the Syrian King wrote a letter on Naaman's behalf to the King of Israel. It also gives specific details about how much money he packed up to bring with him. It is also important to note that the story includes how many changes of clothes that Naaman took with him. Certainly, we can also infer that healing required him to travel.

The very first thing that you need to know is healing requires power and authority to be accessed. You are most likely not able to access it on your own and need someone to make intercession for you. This is essentially what the king of Syria was doing when he wrote the letter. When someone uses their authority and power to access something on your behalf—that is intercession. If there is not a physical person currently assigned to your life making intercession on your behalf, we are assured that Jesus, the Son of God is seated in Heaven on the right side of Abba interceding for you now and always.

The next thing to note is that Naaman took a massive amount of money with him. He understood that it was right and customary to show up before a king and prophet with an offering of high value. The offering should be reflective of the thing that you sought or at least the heart in which you are coming to ask with. His sum of money indicated that he was desperate for healing and he knew that it had that much value. Truthfully, you may not show up with physical money to begin your healing, but you have to be postured to sacrifice whatever you can in order to attain it. Also, we must know that healing costs in general. Naaman's king most likely is the one who resourced him to bring that kind of money.

Jesus, Our King, paid for our healing with His blood. He paid the cost out of the treasury of his life. It is too precious for us not to attain it. Heaven did not spend its best for us to remain in the broken conditions that we may find ourselves in.

The scripture is specific to mention that Naaman packed ten changes of clothes to take with him on his journey. There was no mention of how long the journey was to get there and back or how much time he would be there. However, what these ten changes of clothes represented to me was Naaman's preparation for change and the potential time it could have taken for the change to happen. Anytime we approach a season of healing, we have to be prepared for the changes that can potentially happen. We have to be prepared to take the time. Healing will cost you time.

Lastly, we know that in order for Naaman to be healed, he had to leave Syria and travel to Israel. The grace for his healing was not in his household, his family, his city, his job, or even his nation for that matter. Just like Naaman, when you become ready for healing—just desperate enough—you may be required to move out of everything that is familiar to you. Often times your comfort zone is a petri dish that hosts the things that are contaminating your soul. It is the incubator for your continuation in pain and dysfunction. God will begin to call you out and separate you from the things that you are used to. He may have you physically move. He also may have you emotionally and mentally relocate so that you can be away from certain people and environments. He is setting you up to walk right into the atmosphere most conducive for you to get to the healing waters. You need to know that healing will cost you your comfort.

Healing simply isn't free. It costs God and us something and should be assigned its proper value in your heart.

QUALIFIED HEALERS

We move deeper into Naaman's story and we see that the letter that was sent out was troubling to the King of Israel. The King of Syria addressed the highest-ranking authority in the region to access healing for Naaman, but he was not the one anointed to heal him. It is important to pay attention to this for this reason: to distinguish gifts, graces, and skillsets meant for our time of healing.

A major principle we need to gather is that, we must be able to discern who is anointed and skilled for us. We cannot get caught up in stature and assume that the person who is the highest ranking has the grace to take us where we need to go. You need to hear the Lord and allow him to identify the person He has graced to help you deal with your pain and hurt. Elijah knew he was the man for the job. The King was completely thrown into a frantic episode because he was not prepared to take on the work of healing. A person of great authority without the grace to handle you can further damage you. You have to be mindful of the relationship alignments that you make in seasons of healing or when you feel the pressure of an impending journey to healing. You have to abandon your normal ambition and common practice of rubbing elbows with those who appear to be the "who's who" in your sphere. You have to listen, watch, and discern. Wait on the Lord to dispatch the qualified healers.

I would like to also insert a small caveat for those who are in positions of spiritual authority. It is important that you are integral about your grace, gifts, skills, and assignments. If you know that you are not equipped to walk a person through their healing, be honest with them. Do not subject them to your malpractice. The blood will be on your hands. You will have to answer to God for the further damage that you cause. The reality is that we are not called to everyone and nor are we graced to do the same thing for every person in our jurisdiction. Embrace that truth and everyone will be better in the end.

MIND YOUR P's

Naaman's story continues to get more and more interesting. The principles that we extract get furthermore intense. You have to allow the Lord to lead your journey of healing. You cannot assume the way that he will take. It is important that on the journey to healing that you don't try to plot and navigate your own course. Your responsibility is to submit and respond to the voice of the Lord. Naaman almost forfeited his healing because he did not want to yield to the Lord's way. The Lord gave me a simple way to help navigate through some of the challenges that may come up while on the journey. I say it like this, "Mind your P's!" Let me list and explain what the "P's" are. The "P"s are: your preconceptions, preferences, prejudices, phobias, and areas of pride, These are all areas that you need to be most careful with or they can halt you mid-stride as you move toward the healing waters that are sure to wash over your life.

Preconceptions

The story continues to say that Elijah summoned Naaman to his house and then sent a messenger outside to tell him to go wash in the Jordan River seven times and he would be clean and restored. It then says that Naaman was angry because he **surely** thought that the Prophet Elijah would come outside and stand in front of him and wave his hands over him and cure him that way. Naaman's preconceived notion made him almost miss his chance for healing. He assumed that because he heard or saw that Elijah had used a certain method with someone before that it was going to be done the same for him. He was so sure that he was angry when it did not happen that way. He was so mad that he started out on a path to leave. How easy would it be for us to miss the very thing that God has for us because it did not show up the way that we assumed it should be? How often do we create an atmosphere of disappointment and anger with God because we have obligated him to our imagined expectations? We simply need to yield and only expect what God directly tells us in the journey. Listen and yield your heart.

Preferences

Within the context of the same part of the story, Naaman says to Elijah's servant, "Are not Abana and Pharpar, the rivers of Damascus, better than all the waters of Israel? Could I not wash in them and be clean?" How arrogant? I mean this really has to be the worse time ever to insert his preference. All things considered, the Jordan was known for being a pretty dirty river. However, if Elijah—being the voice of God in this scenario—says specifically to do something, we should immediately obey if we are really that desperate to be healed. Many people miss out on healing when we choose to avoid the treatment because it falls outside of the lines of our preferences. We cannot afford to be *spoiled* or entitled on this journey. If we truly want to be healed, we cannot let our preferences hinder us.

Prejudices

Additionally, we cannot assume that we have all the information about something or someone and judge unrighteously. We will run the risk of disqualifying ourselves from receiving from them. When we are accustomed to things being a certain way or being surrounded by certain kinds of people, we may have difficulty receiving from people and/or things that live outside of what we consider comfortable. We have to be mindful to not be prejudice. The thing or people who are least like you may be the very thing that God uses to usher you in to your greatest breakthroughs in healing.

Phobias

Most often, in the process of healing and on the journey thereof, we have to confront our history and ourselves. This can be a very scary experience. Simultaneously, God introduces new people, places, and environments while taking us to unknown destinations. All of this can be very troublesome for an already fragile heart. Fear manifests in all kinds of ways. Most time we see people expressing fear but it looks like anger or some other secondary emotion. Fear's goal is to keep you from doing whatever it is that makes you uncomfortable. You have to face your fears and lean deeply into the love of God to walk through what feels like darkness. Don't yield to that feeling of paralysis that tells you to stop or quit. Many people forgo healing because they fear the method of its administration. I am telling you to not lose heart. You will be rewarded for your courage.

Pride

Much of what we see manifest in Naaman in this middle part of his story is as a result of pride. Pride is like a scale that is auto-projected to protect a lie in the heart. Pride will make you think its ok to be dysfunctional. Pride will make you think that you know better than what God knows when He is the one that is doing the healing. Pride will make you feel like you are too good or better than what and where you are. I tell you though, PRIDE IS A LIAR. It is a false reality. It is an alternate universe when comparing it to the real world of your existence. Pride will make you keep your pain and tell you that there is absolutely nothing wrong. I tell you that you absolutely have to come out of agreement with pride and allow the truth to blow up the lies in your heart if you are ever going to be whole and unhindered to heal.

If you are able to wrestle with your preconceptions, preferences, prejudice, phobias, and pride to allow the Spirit of God to have his way, you will be able to make it to the healing waters. You will be able to get back on the path and continue the journey.

COMPANY YOU KEEP

Naaman's journey would not have ended in the way that we have come to know it had it not been for the anointed people in his company. It would have been a story of tragedy if he had immature and *petty* people connected to him. We have to be extremely careful about the people that we keep in our inner circle at these most vulnerable seasons when healing is pending. Those relationships can absolutely make or break your journey. The story records Naaman's servants challenging his response to the word given to him. They did not just support his immature response. Many of us think that we have "ride or die" relationships because they go along with everything that we do. However, it is my opinion that people like that really don't love you at all. Who sees a loved one in danger and says nothing? AN ENEMY! Your inner circle should be able to tell you that you are out of line. If no one in your circle is currently able to do that, you need to reevaluate who is there and the reasons why.

Those servants did not just challenge him but they also were able to bring back the Word of God to him.

Do you have people in your inner circle that can help you hear and remember what God has spoken to you? Do you have people that can remember what you have been praying for and announce its arrival? These are the kinds of people you need in your circle. These are the kinds of people that God used to bring Naaman to the final step to apprehend his healing.

The company you keep is very important on any occasion but it has the greatest severity when you are crossing over thresholds of healing and deliverance. Your company can be the thing God uses to get you into the river.

STAY IN THE WATER

The last and final stage of Naaman's story is probably the most significant. This is the stage that we can get to and completely blow the whole journey into smithereens. It's not the glaring things that can make it all go terrible. It's the subtle missteps that can be most detrimental. The story goes on to say that Naaman eventually went to the Jordan and dipped seven times and his flesh was restored like that of a child. Naaman was fully obedient in the end of the story. He made it to the healing waters and applied them just as he was instructed to.

The truth is that many of us are not always inclined to follow the instruction all the way through until the end. Suppose Naaman went to Jordan and dipped one time and got out. Many of us would have done this. We would feel like the water itself has the ability to heal and one dip would just do it. We may become overwhelm with the initial immersion and just declare that it was enough and has done its job. We have to know that we cannot prematurely abort the journey because we simply feel differently in a moment. What if Naaman dipped five times and saw visible changes and decided to get out? He would not have fully been restored as God intended. At the initial tangible encounter with the grace power of God, (5 biblically represents grace) we cannot get so overwhelm that we don't endure the healing through to completion (7 biblically represents completion and wholeness). You see, leprosy had so many effects and the Lord had to heal everything. We have to be cautious not to prematurely jump out of the healing waters right before the process is complete. We can put ourselves at risk of going back to the state we were in. God had to deal with all of those *bacteria* that had taken over his whole life and he has to do the same thing to us. In healing, almost never counts. It's either all the way or not at all. Completion reflects God's faithfulness. The story says that Naaman fully dipped seven times until he was restored to that of a child. We have to allow God to restore our souls to the state that it was in when we innocent children—before the trauma and terrible experiences. You owe it to yourself to stay in the water once you get there. Don't come out until you look like the version of yourself that God made.

ONWARD TO HEALING

Naaman's life is a perfect case study for us to see the overview of where God is taking us. You may still be

Naaman in Syria just now feeling the weight of your pain. You may be Naaman finding out that there is help for you. You may be Naaman preparing for the journey toward healing. You may be Naaman working through your P's. You may be Naaman stepping in the water. It doesn't matter where you locate yourself in this story—one thing remains true: God wants you unhindered to move toward your river. He wants to help remove any and everything that is in your path between you and your life being perfectly immersed into His healing waters. My prayer is that you don't faint and fully embrace this journey that is ahead. Over the next several chapters, we will explore some very practical wisdom that I believe will convey spiritual truths that help you prepare for or stay the course on your Journey. Listen to the wisdom of Abba speak to your heart.

Journey Thoughts | Chapter 1

1. Do you identify with the principles of Naaman's journey?
2. What are some things that you have done to avoid hidden pain?
3. Have you heard wisdom from unusual places and people lately about healing?
4. Are you ready to pay the cost and do the work for your inner healing?
5. Do you believe that God is concerned about your inner healing?
6. Who is someone in your life that you believe is qualified to walk with you through your healing journey?
7. Of the P's, which of them do you think presents the greatest challenge for you?
8. When you survey your current inner circle, are these people who will really be able to support you as you heal? Are there changes that need to be made?
9. In the past, have you started a healing journey and prematurely ended it? What are some safeguards that can keep you from doing that again?

Part 2
Wisdom on the Way

JOURNEY TO THE RIVER

Chapter 2 – Time is Relative

Following the spiritual insight of Naaman's journey gives us all a prophetic picture of the journey that one may take to get back to wholeness. Naaman had a point in life where God-ordained pressure contracted all around him to thrust him into wholeness. All of the accouterments of life were seemingly in place for him, but the journey he needed to take was to address a part of him that was personal and specific. You, like Naaman, are most likely entering into that season or are soon to be coming upon it. As you are being prepared to start your journey to the river, I want to offer you some very practical wisdom. Over the next several chapters, I want to help you prepare for the things that you may face along the way so that you can endure the journey ahead.

THROW AWAY YOUR CLOCK

The very first piece of wisdom I want to offer to you is: *THROW AWAY YOUR CLOCK*. Please, go ahead and do yourself a favor. This journey will not fit into any preconceived notion that you have about the pace that this process should adhere to. You mostly likely won't try to slowdown the healing process. (It's easy to rush when it comes to facing the difficult parts of life.) All of healing's nuances and challenges will cause you to want to speed it up though. Here's some advice: DON'T GET IN A RUSH. You cannot expedite God's process through your impatience because longsuffering (patience) is one of His greatest characteristics. He knows just how much you can handle at one time. Besides, your soul is a quality creation and should be treated with care. If you have been through a lifetime of pain, trauma of any kind, or any significant hurt, your heart will not be repaired in a day.

   I would caution you to not even pay attention to *chronos time (*time measured in minutes, hours and days). You will be better off assessing kairos time (time measured by quality—synchronized with Abba's perfect moments). In fact, the kairos moment is coming for you to begin your journey to the river. (Reading this book right now is probably a kairos moment.) Staying in sync with the Spirit of God will be the only route to complete success and 100% restoration. I'm not talking about creating the stress of anticipation. You will do nothing for yourself attempting to get ahead of God. "Staying in sync," means only move where His presence has already gone; only do what He has given you strength and grace to do; and lean and stand in areas that are staffed with your supporting cast curated by Him.

Do not allow your heart to be kidnapped by "should". That's the phase when you lean into a lot of misinformed presuppositions about healing. You might say things like, "I *should* be done with this by now." "This *should* be easier." "This *should* not effect me like this." "This *should* not take this long." "I *should* not even be bothered by this." "I *should* just get over it." None of that is helpful. You *should* relax and allow Abba to lead you. Patience is a virtue and you will need to have it mostly for yourself on this journey.

The journey will have cyclical parts. Some things you will feel like you have had to address and revisit multiple times. You have to understand that Abba will address certain areas of your hurt in parts. Each time, He may address a different level. Don't think that you are losing time because things have to be done in steps. Everything on this journey will be interconnected. Remember that, even when Abba has you in places that feel like they have no connection to the destination. He is a masterful guide in healing and leading His people to wholeness.

RELATIVITY

Another very important nugget of wisdom is: FOCUS YOUR EYES. This is actually something that you should regularly do in life anyway. It is even more important to do when you begin your journey to the river. Healing requires exposure and causes vulnerability. Vulnerability makes you open and in that state you tend to notice everything that is happening around you in a hypersensitive fashion. You experience most things in extremes. When you are hurt, you also don't see with clarity and most times aren't looking at the right things. You pay a lot of attention to other people. I believe it's our way of leveling out the discomfort that we feel. However, you can immediately move into a dangerous game of comparison. You will start measuring your progress or wellness by comparing it what you see in other people. Most of what you see is a facade. Collectively, we tend to not consider processes and only look at presented results. This is so dangerous to do when we are attempting to heal.

The relativity of time should be considered as you prepare for your journey. Occupying the same time and space with people does not automatically suggest that they are experiencing things in the time frame that you perceive. Nothing is as it appears—especially when it comes to timing or healing. Sharing identical trauma and pain and approaching the healing journey in tandem with a person still would not result in an identical healing time. Only by supernatural effort can two people occupy the exact time frame together. Individually, we experience time through internal pace and pressure. How something impacts you will be different than the next person. How you experience life will be completely different than those outside of your life frame. The slightest difference in context can completely differentiate the experience of healing. I have a great personal story that will help illustrate the point I'm making.

PIERCED

One Thanksgiving holiday, I went to visit my sister. She had been trying to get me to get matching tattoos with her for a long time. I could not bring myself to sign up AND PAY for that kind of pain. That weekend, she was still determined to get me to do it. I wouldn't budge on it and she eventually became weary of my *no's*. Her consolation was for us to get matching piercings. I had been contemplating getting an upper ear piercing and she was equally cool with it. It was going be quick and essentially painless, especially in comparison to getting a tattoo. So we went to the mall after our Friday Thanksgiving meal. We walked into Claire's fully invested in our sisterly bond. We told the clerk why we were there. They gave us the formal information for piercings and the after care. We had to pay and sign a waiver. We had the exact same technician. She marked both of ears on the same side. We had the same starting earrings. She used the exact same gun to pierce both of us. She did the exact same steps for clean up. We both equally felt like it was quick and easy. The service ended with her telling us that the healing window was around 6 weeks. We left there with the understanding that we would have a little *touching tenderness* over the next several days. We left knowing that we had to clean our piercing site twice per day and rotate the earrings. We left with our twin piercings, supplies and smiles in tow.

While getting into the truck to leave, my foot slipped. My body went forward and I banged that newly pierced site on the doorframe. It hurt a bit but it was ok after several minutes. Over the course of the weekend, I believe my sister got her shirt caught on the earring while getting dressed. It pulled on the sensitive site, but she was fine after a few minutes. We carried on with our weekend and for the most part didn't have any other issues.

After I returned home and life resumed its regularity, we would do our normal sister check in as usual. Only this time, we would alternate asking the other one about issues with pain and inflammation from the piercing. We almost never experienced the same problems at the same time. If my ear was hurting or swollen and hers wasn't, I immediately questioned the healing process. There is a lot of wisdom that I extracted from this experience. In those moments of difference, I did not take into consideration the relativity of time. Our pain was the same and was caused by the same exact thing. It also almost happened at the exact same time. However, our pace and pressures were different. This meant that we had different factors to consider in our healing journey—well, journeys because although they happened together, they were separate experiences.

She worked in a hospital and I had a more physically demanding job. This immediately could add elements to the healing process that we did not think about. We cannot compare our experiences in healing with other people (no matter their emotional proximity) because we don't know the personal demands they have while navigating their journey. Those demands can have great impact on the pace they are able to maintain. The demands of life can have pressures of differing intensities at different times. Their context determines all of that and is a very critical consideration for the healing journey. All of this will effect how and when a person heals.

My sister and I both had different experiences during that initial weekend where we injured a freshly pierced site. Everyone has different pain tolerance thresholds. This will determine how much can be handled within the healing process without impairing forward momentum. You must also understand that your tolerance for pain doesn't lessen its impact on the pace of the journey. You can have the ability to manage pain but the damage it causes still requires more healing time. You don't know how those kinds of things can negatively impact the healing process. Those two incidents (and I'm sure there were so many more over the next few weeks) certainly could have added time to the healing journey. We did not factor it in during those conversations. As anyone sets out on their journey to the river, life is still happening and incidents and accidents occur. This all has to be considered along the way.

Another thing to note is that we also had different sleeping habits. When sleeping on my stomach, I favored the side of my pierced ear. She slept opposite of that. A person's resting habits will be severely exposed when heading to the river and can have an effect on the healing time. Take into account that you may not have learned how to lean away from pain. Your version of rest may include adding unnecessary stress and pressure out of habit. As you heal, you will have to learn how to lean in to the bosom of the Father instead of your usual bed of pain.

While considering habits, we also both had lapses in adhering to the cleaning guidelines. As I stated before, it was supposed to be twice daily. We started off good, but demands on our schedules caused both of us to be inconsistent at different times. In fact, the closer we got to the presumed healing date (6 weeks), we kind of felt like it was unnecessary. Of course, we were wrong. In the healing journey sometimes, we will cause additional pain because we choose not to follow God's instructions. As you prepare for your journey, let me admonish you to LISTEN and OBEY all the way through to the end. Don't get too busy or too lazy to keep up whatever disciplines are required for your specific process. Your leaning toward inconsistency can prolong your healing. Don't assume that you are done because you don't feel like you used to. Taking shortcuts can ultimately lengthen the journey to the river.

TIME REVEALS

We finally reached about 6 weeks and a few days and I was ready to change my earring from a stud to a hoop. For the days leading up to that, I had no pain. I felt fine. I just knew that the healing process was over. I walked into the bathroom and begin to remove the earring from my upper ear. In order to do so, I had to apply a little pressure to take the earring back off. It was pretty snug. I got the earring out and attempted to put the new earring in. My ear was so swollen that I almost could not get the new earring in and get the back affixed. By the time I was done, my ear was shooting with pain. You see, time and pressure revealed to me that my ear was not yet healed. This is why it's important to follow God all the way through the process. It will keep us from making faulty assumptions about where we are in our journey. The saying goes "time heals all wounds." I can't say that I agree with that. If nothing else, time will reveal many things about you and your wounds. In this case, our need to follow a ready-made healing schedule will push us to add pressures ahead of His perfect plan.

TIME IS UNIQUE

Even worse, we attempt to fit our healing into some cookie-cutter schematic to somehow keep up with other people. We think we have to do it in *this* amount of time because we perceived that someone else did. We push our healing schedules to keep up with what we perceive to be happening around us. I reiterate, "perceive" because much of what we are looking at is not as it appears. We get in a rush to get back to *business as usual* only to find that it's nothing there for us. I grew extremely frustrated because I was told that *everyone else* healed in about 6 weeks and I was still in pain. The technician was not trying to mislead me, she simply told me what she was taught. How many people do you know report back to their piercing technicians to give them an update on their healing process after 6 weeks? (I've never met one.) Let's just say ear cartilage has some scientifically proven healing rate—they aren't as uniquely made as souls. The amount of time it takes is unique from person to person. How your soul heals and what it needs for healing is very specific to you and orchestrated by God. Having false timing makes you create false deadlines for the process. False deadlines create false hope and ultimately leads to disappointment. This cycle has to be avoided because it has the ability to make you quit on your way. When you appoint something to happen at a certain time in your heart and it doesn't happen as you plan, disappointment sets in. Disappointment can lead to despair and hopelessness. Hope is what makes you endure to the end. Staying in sync with God is the only thing that stabilizes your hope. You need stable hope to endure your journey. You need hope to make it to a place that you have never been before. You need hope to surrender to a process that you will not be completely in charge of.

WHOLENESS IS THE GOAL

As I said, time is relative. You can only absolutely agree with a timeline when you share the exact same reference point. The only reference point that should matter on this journey is the one who sits high and looks low: Abba. He has it all in his hands—including the timing of your journey. He has already accounted for your missteps, pauses, detours, and stagnation. His grace will pull you through all of that and he can reconcile it all. The focus has to only be your responsibility to the goal. The most important part of the ear-piercing story is that my ear healed. No it did not heal at the same time as the average person. I did not even heal at the exact same time as my sister. None of that mattered. When I focused on doing what was necessary to complete the journey, my healing came. So in terms of time, my last bit of wisdom is: KEEP YOUR EYES OFF OF THE CLOCK AND TOWARD YOUR WHOLENESS. Look alive!! There is a river ahead.

Journey Thoughts | Chapter 2

1. Are you an impatient person? Are you more impatient with yourself or others?
2. What impact does timing have on your ability to focus?
3. How do you plan to get in sync with God on a daily basis?
4. What are some internal *should* statements that you know you need to rid yourself of to start this journey?
5. Do you often compare yourself to others? (Success, failures, possessions, etc.)
6. What are some boundaries that you can set in place, while healing, to help focus your eyes?
7. What is an area that you once believed was healed but time revealed that deeper healing is needed?

JOURNEY TO THE RIVER

Chapter 3 – Avoiding Soul Placebos

PLACEBOS. WHAT IS THAT?

Settling the issue of time, this journey to healing will be quite adventurous. There are so many things that will try to intrude the path to the water. In fact, there are things that can emerge that may make us think we don't need to get to the river. Abba would not be a good father if he did not give us some precautions to watch out for as we move forward. The thing that he wants us to do at this juncture is to avoid *soul placebos*. This is a pretty heavy precaution because it is the thing that trips most of us up when we become too overwhelmed with the pain that comes with healing. Before we deeply dive into the fullness of this, let's discuss what a placebo is. A placebo is basically any treatment that you get that has no real value. In medicine, it is common to give a placebo in the form of a sugar tab. It is generally used to test the effectiveness of a new medication. Medical professionals have a group of patients with a similar medical challenge. They split the group into three. One group is the constant and receives nothing. One group receives the actual treatment. The final group receives a placebo. In some cases, some of the people who receive the placebo would report signs of improved health. They would legitimately feel better because the mind would be tricked into believing that they received a real treatment. Ultimately, that which they received had no medical value and they didn't actually treat the problem.

SOUL PLACEBOS

Now that we have an understanding of a placebo in the traditional sense, let me breakdown the soul placebo. Like the medical placebo, a soul placebo is anything that we would substitute to make us feel better in the place of genuine healing. As we go through life with our emotional hurts, we can get pretty desperate to numb the pain. Unlike the natural placebo that is normally administered for testing, soul placebos are sought after alternatives to the real thing. The things that we put into place to cover our pain have no real value to our souls. Soul placebos can vary person to person based upon preferences, proclivities, iniquities, familiar spirits, accessibility, opportunities, and the like.

Some people choose mood-altering substances like drugs and/or alcohol to escape their pain. They can potentially provide a temporary escape from the weight of the pain. People want to escape their reality by "getting high" or "getting faded". The hard part about this kind of placebo is that you always have to come back to the reality that you temporarily escape. For a false sense of permanent escape, people will repetitively consume these products. Therein starts the cycle of addiction. Now, on top of the hurt that he or she has attempted to mask, they also now have a substance abuse issue and all of the challenges that come with it. As we stated earlier, there is not real value added to the soul with this soul placebo.

Others pursue relationships and sex to try to run away from pain. Have you witness someone who was a serial dater? Maybe you are that person. Most times people in pain pursue relationships as a distraction and not out of love. A person in emotional turmoil hardly ever wants to be alone with their feelings. They don't really want to face the harsh reality of their condition so they borrow the lives of others to get lost in. The only problem is this is not as soul soothing as they hoped it would be. Whatever relief they get is only temporary. The reason for that is because all humans have pain. It is only a matter of time before the problems of the other person's life collides with the person that is running from theirs. These relationships can vary from platonic, romantic, spiritual, to extremely causal. The type of relationship doesn't matter. It is the borrowed energy that matters. Once the hurt person realizes that the honeymoon phase of the relationship is over, they often fizzle out and look for a new relationship to entertain. Sometimes this is acted out through exclusively sexual relationships. Sex provides a chemical release that can boost the mood. Hurt people can easily become sex addicts or sexual abusers because they use sex like other people use drugs. Sex is simply a means of escape. There is no intention of building a bond or sharing intimacy with their sexual partners. They simply engage in the act to try to access that chemical release and neurological stimulation to temporarily distract them from the low state they regularly have to exist in. Again, these both have no true value when it comes to healing the soul from years of unearthed pain. Ultimately, both of these things can further compound the problem because of the exchanges that are had while dealing with so many people. Sex was never meant to be trivial for spiritual beings. There is no need to buy into this animalistic perspective that says that you can engage in sexual acts without any emotional or spiritual consequence. The same can be said about engaging with the souls of other people while expecting no residue of their life to be left on you and vice versa.

Another soul placebo that is used, but not talked about as much, is FOOD! Food provides a chemical release in the same way that the other examples do. Many people develop very unhealthy eating habits and answer all callings to cravings without even a hint of self-control. There are extreme cases of overeating and emotional eating. Most people indulge in what we call "comfort food" or foods that provide the very least nutritional value. Food, consumed unhealthily, leads to weight gain and other health challenges. Emotional issues lead people to food addictions. Food addicts can live very debilitating lives just like alcoholics, drug addicts, and sex addicts. When you see people who literally are immobile from the weight, you are most likely looking at a person with a life filled with emotionally traumatic experiences. (This does not apply to every person that struggles with obesity. There are other medical conditions that cause this problem as well.) Like all of the other soul placebos, food may provide a temporary mental escape but only further complicates the problem and pains that you originally had.

There are many other soul placebos but I will bring up one more: MONEY! How it's spent, when it spent, why it's spent, and how much all can convey a very detailed story about state of your soul. Many people use money to fulfill they same high as the other soul placebos. Money is an expression of power and control or the lack thereof. Wild episodes with splurging, gambling, and unrestricted buying can create an alternate reality for a short minute. It's expensive, yet, has no real value. In all of that spending, peace for the soul cannot be purchased. The hard part about soul placebos is that they all have lows and negative consequences. When the person comes to a moment of sobriety and realizes they have spent the money they needed for their responsibilities, a deeper low sets in. There is no place to escape in this false sense of healing.

DECEPTION NEVER HEALS YOU

As you can see, soul placebos are far more dangerous than medical placebos. Medical placebos have the potential to trick the mind of a person into thinking they are better. (Ex. The pain of a headache can potentially dissipate because of the placebo effect.) This is not that big of a deal in medicine, because it is most often administered in a controlled environment. The medical professional generally monitors the actual condition of the body and provides real treatment when needed. When it comes to the soul, placebos are a form of deception. Deception blinds you to the world that you actually exist in. Soul placebos can create an alternate reality that you can be lost in. You may not be able to identify it in yourself; however, all of us have seen someone in this state. We often wonder if they can really see themselves or hear themselves. This is why Abba warns us to avoid soul placebos. There is no way to begin the healing journey for a condition that you are blind to. This is the ultimate danger of engaging in soul placebos. The first thing that you must do is to completely surrender your placebos if you want to be healed. As I already stated, soul placebos cause deception. When you are in deception concerning the condition of your soul—especially emotionally—you hinder yourself from healing. You may be wondering how this is true. Let us look deeper at the specific dangers of soul placebos.

DANGERS OF PLACEBOS

Soul placebos are probably more damming to you than the original pain. The placebos ultimately give you a false peace and comfort. You can begin to really think you are getting better. The placebos can cause you to suppress your pain. We know that pain does not just disappear. It embeds itself causing a negative mutation to the very thing it is attached to. You are doing yourself no favors by trying to avoid addressing that hurt in your heart. You are actually hurting yourself worse. The placebos that you are engaging in have grave consequence to your soul. There are three specific ones that I would like to explain here: disarming symptoms, destiny derailment, and dying in dysfunction.

The consequential fallouts of engaging in soul placebos are all of heightened importance. However, I can't help but notice their cyclical relationship one to another. We ultimately know soul placebos are forms of deception. To the sick heart, not having clarity about what really is happening internally is the thing that keeps you sick. This brings me to the very first consequence of soul placebos: **disarming symptoms.** Deception has the power to conceal the indicators that let you know you are not well. Let's be real—no one likes to experience symptoms of any kind of sickness, but without them there is no way to know you are in danger. In my opinion, emotional sickness is far worse than physical sickness. Why? Emotional sickness can completely disable you through your heart and mind. Then, if untreated, it can progressively seep out of your heart and begins to impact the physical body. Now, for the things that you may be able press through and do because of your emotional and mental fortitude, your physical body now has limitations and hinders you. We absolutely need symptoms to communicate as they were designed to. I heard a physical trainer say, in jest, "Pain won't kill you. It actually lets you know you are alive."

The goal is to get you to begin your journey so a simpler prophetic image of this is the alert system in your car. If the gas needle was not calibrated to respond to the pressure in the gas tank, there would be no way to tell if the car was about to run out of gas. You would never know how much gas to put in the car either. This is terribly dangerous. Now, imagine if that gas needle corresponded to a significant function of your soul. Taking a soul placebo would cause the gas needle to not correspond to what is actually in the tank. Soul placebos will have you thinking you are full when you are empty. Let's say a symptom still tries to push through to certain degree. Have in mind; symptoms are your alert system. If the symptom has been interfered with in anyway, it will no longer give enough information, give correction information, or give needed information at the right time. All of these functions need to be in place to provide you the best opportunity to stop a pending issues or recover after an issue is presented. Disarming symptoms is like purposely breaking the *gas needle* of your heart.

As already stated, disarming symptoms is a powerful fall out of engaging in soul placebos, but it is not necessarily the worse of the three. It is the beginning of a devastating cycle. This brings me to the next piece in the chain of events: **destiny derailment.** Your destiny is the manifested totality of everything that God intends for you to become. If we continue with the car example, the gas needle being broken is not that bad. You can become pretty familiar with this level of malfunctioning and determine a safe time to put some *gas* back in your car. The thing that you have to be mindful of is that you are completely taking a shot in the dark. You may make many missteps trying to figure out timing and accuracy when its time to address things. With the alert system intact, you would know if you needed to take a break (to go the river). But, just like a car, if we don't have what we need at the right time, we will find ourselves broken down. There is no forward momentum or ability to accelerate toward our destiny. We can't even start anything new without first addressing the issue. In your life, I am pretty sure you have seen distressed vehicles left on the side of the road temporarily. It is possible the owner of the vehicle had a broken gas needle and ran out of gas. They may have had some other minor issues that were still reparable. Nonetheless, they were hindered from making progress at that time. This is what our lives look like in this cycle. We ignore, suppress or interfere with our alert system and miss important signals that eventually lead us to derailment and breakdown. Breakdown causes delay no matter how you slice it. This is a serious matter when it comes to your destiny. The redeeming thing is that derailments don't have to be permanent problems. If we address the immediate need and restore the alert system, we can get back on the road to destiny. Sadly enough, though, most people in this cycle caused by soul placebos don't restore the system. They apply patchwork to the immediate problem. They only address what is urgent and go further into the gravest part of the cycle.

The final phase of the cycle is **dying in dysfunction.** The truth is, what you don't heal can kill you. We are programmed to believe that if you ignore a problem it will go away. We have seen this thought played out so many times. It is most obvious when we talk about physical sickness. The lack of visibility, as it pertains to the soul, does not change the level of significance. This is what makes this the gravest part of the cycle. You can literally die to your destiny before you physically die if you do not heal as Abba intended. To return to the car analogy, when this point is reached—cars are abandoned or simply used for it parts.

Abandoned cars just sit idle and never do what they were designed to do. This is a prophetic picture of your life as it pertains to God's destiny when you continue to engage soul placebos. This is an extremely depressing way to live out the rest of your days. I absolutely believe that being "used for parts" is far more egregious. To not live out the very thing you're made for is torturous at the very least. To exist in fragments of this reality is a tragedy. What does this look like? Let's say your destiny was for you to become a restaurateur that owned and establish a few different successful restaurant chains. Because you were trapped in your dysfunction, you tragically live out the rest of your life cooking in a fast food restaurant. (Note: there is nothing wrong with cooking at a fast food place in general.) I guess I am an all or nothing kind of person. I'd rather not be around something than to witness glimpses of it and not be allowed to ever experience it in its fullest expression. This, to me, is the epitome of dying a million deaths. Dying in your dysfunction is the worse possible outcome that a human can experience. Again, I am not even talking about dying physically. There are far worse ways to die. The cycle of soul placebos produces no wins.

If you are in the cycle, there is still hope. You can still be reset by the power of God. You may not have successfully avoided soul placebos but you now have an option to abandon them. You can see where they lead. Abba wants you to have his best. Soul placebos are a hindrance to your healing journey. What you don't address in your soul and emotions will be duplicated. What you don't conquer, your children will face and be ill equipped to overcome. The need for healing is not just about you. It is for the next generation. Dig deep! Avoid or completely abandon these soul placebos so you can soberly, honestly, and vulnerably begin the journey to the river.

Journey Thoughts | Chapter 3

1. Are you able to see the use of soul placebos in your life?
2. Do you find that you consume alcohol, drugs, or other substances to manage yourself?
3. Do you healthily engage in new relationships with people and places? Do you notice a pattern of quick entry and quit exit in new relationships?
4. If you are not married, do you have multiple casual sexual relationships and you know it's not the lifestyle that you want to lead?
5. What is your relationship with food? What is your motivation for its consumption?
6. Is your eating secretive or often in over-indulgence beyond control? Has is created a weight problem?
7. How do you use money? Are your spending habits connected to your mood?
8. If you pulled up your bank statement, does it reflect responsibility or frivolity?
9. Have you fallen into the cycle of deception that comes from using soul placebos?
10. Do you believe you have the courage to lay them down to soberly start your true healing journey?

JOURNEY TO THE RIVER

Chapter 4 – Symptoms Speak

POWERFUL REVELATORS

As you have walked through the importance of avoiding soul placebos, you may realize that the symptoms you intended to avoid will eventually have to fully come to the surface. I know this is a scary position to be in because that is essentially why you went to the soul placebos in the first place. Your deep hurts began to show up in your life in ways that you were not ready to deal with. With all of your soul placebos relinquished, the offshoots or symptoms from your deeply rooted issues become paramount and feel seemingly unbearable. Honestly, I know it's very difficult to be soberly face to face with all of that pain. It's very hard, but you need to do this. You need your symptoms to come through without interruption. You need to let all of them speak to you and through you. In the journey to the river, symptoms are powerful revelators and communicators. The revelation of your symptoms always precedes diagnosis. My wisdom to you here is to LET THEM SPEAK.

When you are experiencing symptoms in your physical body, at home or in your comfort zone, you immediately want to take something to just get rid of it. This is problematic over time because you do not know what is causing that symptom to show up in the first place. This behavior trend could be detrimental. If you translate this to your emotional health, ultimately you imprison yourself in a fortress of pain because there is no true medicine powerful enough to make you "get over" the hurt and trauma in the heart. You have to go through the healing process. Letting the symptoms speak is a part of that journey.

When you go to seek medical attention, the attending physician always asks you about the symptoms that bring you into their office. They are not asking you this question to be nosey or to waste time. Symptoms give them information that can lead to treating the real issue. Our natural bend often leads us to medicate the symptoms that are most pressing or most obvious while ignoring the more covert ones and the ones that emerge in our blind spots. Ultimately, medicating some symptoms and leaving others in play often lead to misdiagnosis. Don't take yourself out of the process because of the discomfort of the symptoms you are experiencing. Symptoms are informational no matter how inconvenient or uncomfortable they may feel.

Let's say that you are constantly fatigue. You literally only want to sleep and lay around. You may go out to do only the necessities, but you immediately return home to get in your bed or place of comfort. Now some people will start ingesting inordinate amounts of caffeine. Others move on to heavier substances to boost their energy levels. The problem with this is eventually the desire to sleep may not be present, but an addiction to the substances becomes the new issue. Truthfully, this symptom could point to issues with anemia, a problematic thyroid, a dysfunctional pituitary gland, or other serious conditions. If you would actually pause and investigate what that symptom was communicating, you could be a lot closer to healing the problem. We have to get out of swatting at flies while leaving the *stink* in our lives.

ROOT CAUSE ANALYSIS

We don't only do these things as it pertains to our physical body. We often and especially do this in matters of the soul. If you are willing to allow the symptoms, they will give you a lot of information. As I said, there is a reason that all doctors or medical professionals ask you about your symptoms upon initial visits. Based on their training, symptoms and their combinations can point toward specific conditions, dysfunctions, or diseases. AFTER gathering information (VERY IMPORTANT TO NOTE), they may try to relieve discomfort by treating symptoms that cause severe issues that disrupt our lives. This is also done to try to rule out simpler issues. However, all good doctors will eventually move to root cause analysis for more complex issues. There is no sense in cutting off branches that will spring back up if the root is still intact.

Abba is the chief physician and operates the same way. It is important to Him that you are aware of why you are how you are. True inner healing cannot begin without identifying the source. Real deliverance cannot happen without identifying the *strong man* (the deepest and most important mindset that governs your life). I urge you to submit all of your *symptoms* to God so that he can take you to the root of an issue. Allow him to fully inspect you. Give Him permission to touch and tap on sensitive areas until the source of your pain is discovered.

Understand that the discovery is not for Him, but it's for you. This is also true for the doctors. The doctor doesn't really benefit from all of the investigative work. He or she could essentially treat the symptoms that you report, bandage you up and send you back home. They would be a well paid professional doing just that. (Actually, some do this.) Going the extra mile is intended to give you the best and most accurate results and overall higher quality of life. In this same manner, God can get use out of you as a fragmented soul, but he chooses to get to the root of things so that you can be whole. He cares that deeply about you. He doesn't want to just use you. He wants you to be His. Everything that is reconciled to Him is a part of Him. He is HOLY (integral, whole) and so His intentions are always to make you just as HE is. However, for this part, your participation is absolutely necessary.

In this space, it's important to move pass just saying, " I just don't trust people." or "I can't help It." or "I'm just mean." or (as a woman saying) "I don't do female friends." Oh, dear heart! You must know that these ideologies are deeply- rooted and provides space for the hurt to remain. You aren't just made this way. You weren't born this way. Although it may have become culturally normal, (within your family culture) that doesn't mean that it is from a healthy place. It is important that you choose not to normalize your symptoms. Allow the discovery process to bring you face to face with truth: THERE IS A PROBLEM.

PERSONALITY OF PAIN

One thing you have to realize is that personality is not static. It's very dynamic and always developing based upon the experiences and exposure of a person. I believe if you know that, you will be ok with hearing that you don't have to be *how* you are. A lot of people believe that they have to stay stuck a certain way because *that's how they've always been*. In the healing process, you will learn that a lot of your personality traits are symptoms of pain, trauma, and dysfunction. You have actually never met or lived as the full version of *whole* you—at least, not yet.

The fear of uncovering your real personality and separating it from the pain of your life can be a weird experience. However, you should not let it hinder you from moving forward with your journey. It is important that you do not allow yourself to move toward a false sense of healing because of fear or discomfort. It is easy to suppress symptoms or soul pains when we just want to get over *it* or get it over with. When you are feeling that way, it's easy to do little work to address the **source** of the pain. I can pretty much guarantee you that all of your little quirky behaviors and irregular preferences and practices have a whole story and history connected to it. Some of it could be trauma. Some of it could be a lie embedded in your heart. Some of it could be a form of protection you developed for yourself. It doesn't matter if its all three—you need to know the truth and you are valuable enough to do the work of healing.

During this time you want to give God all of the things that he puts pressure on and points out. Be completely honest about all of the things that have been manifesting in your life. If you needed a physical doctor to save your life, you would hold nothing back. You would share all of your aches, pains, itches, burns, etc. Do the same in your time with God. It's simple: what is hidden cannot be healed. As I said, the discovery process is for you more than it is for God. You are a partner in this process. Your complete vulnerability is a necessity and is required. It can, indeed, be scary to let all of your brokenness be exposed and seen at once. But this is required to allow the root cause analysis to be completely done.

MANIFESTION PRECEDE DELIVERANCE

You are so accustomed to looking like you have it all together. Most of that is to impress people. You walk around heavy because you live in the context of family, friends, church, work and all of the other parts of your community, but no one knows what's really in your heart. If I'm honest, we all have a representative. (You know…

the version of yourself that you are cool with every knowing but it's not the *real* you.) You are your representative so often, that even you get duped at times by the *front*. Let me put this plainly... find a space to manifest. I mean completely and utterly become raw and undone.

I have yet to come across any deliverance or healing that was not preceded by manifestation. Those accounts of manifestation were not to conclude that God was unaware of the problem without it. In my opinion, manifesting signals a person coming to the end of themselves. It is a relinquishing of the facade. It is a removal of a mask. It is the expression of what was suppressed. It is the actualization of the truth on display. You see, there is no healing without honesty and humility. (In fact, lies incubate disease and dysfunction of the soul and keep us trapped in bondage. But Jesus told us that the TRUTH would set us free.) Every time I saw a full out manifestation, it was in an environment set for healing and deliverance to take place. Honestly, the environment, the season, and the presence of God provoked it to happen.

You need to remember that God is the one who is orchestrating the beginning of your healing journey. It is God that is leading you to those healing waters. It is God that is causing this season of your life to be how it is. He is preparing atmospheres and environments that press and squeeze on you. His goal is to get that pain out of your heart and fill it with himself so that you can be made whole. You may be feeling all the way out of the norm. There is nothing that gratifies or satisfies you. You can't find any comfort in the things that you used to run to for medication and soothing. Trust me when I say, its God's doing. Don't resist him in your attempt to maintain an image. Let your wholeness be your motivation.

FULLY SICK

There is a point in this process where you need to give yourself permission to be full on sick. I mean let all of your soul pain symptoms come to the surface. Listen! Don't neglect the use of wisdom. Choose a safe place for your vulnerability. That may just be between you and God for now. It can be scary because you've never had to come to this place of realness with yourself before. Trust me, though it will be hard, it won't kill you. Don't let the pretentious social media culture pull you out of your process. Don't let poor and unbiblical church cultures make you lie and avoid your brokenness. Be reminded that Jesus's true church has a culture of vulnerability and healing. (James' letter says, "Confess your faults one to another so that you can be healed.") Let me also add that you may want to include a professional. It may be at this point or later in the process. Sometimes, having a skilled and objective therapist helps us get to the root quicker and offers support when it's challenging to face our trauma.

The overall point here is to learn from what is leaking from your soul. Don't ignore it. You've suppressed the experiences. You've medicated the madness. You've run from the reality. None of this changed the truth or healed you. Now, it's time to come face to face with the real issues of your heart. Let the pain give you the information you need so that the Chief Physician can begin your healing process and make you whole. Let the revelation come so that you can be move toward that healing river.

Journey Thoughts | Chapter 4

1. Are you ready to soberly begin your journey?
2. Have you ever allowed yourself to feel the fullness of your pain?
3. What information can you gain from the hidden things in your heart?
4. Do you find it easy to be vulnerable and honest? About your inner most feelings?
5. How do you communicate through pain?
6. Do you currently have a safe place for complete vulnerability?
7. Have you historically shared your pain with God? If no, what has hindered you?
8. Of your personality traits, which of them do you believe may have come because of hurt and past trauma?
9. What do you fear most about allowing your pain to be exposed?
10. Who have you identified as your accountability as you prepare for this process?

JOURNEY TO THE RIVER

Chapter 5 – Own Your Pain

SEEDS & WEEDS

Thank you for continuing with me. I know this is not the easiest thing to do. Let me encourage you, beautiful soul: Life gets better if you allow this wisdom to lead you. It's a pretty big ordeal to really remove all of the things that hinder you from taking your healing journey. One of the greatest things you can do to begin your healing journey is to acknowledge and own your pain. Many people live in a despondent state in response to a life of pain. They often try to put the pain in a separate form apart from the bodies they actually live in. The only problem is, emotional pain is experienced in the soul and then embeds itself in the body when left unattended. The initial blow plants a seed in the heart. Depending on the magnitude of the pain, it is possible that whole gardens of seeds are planted in the heart. They sprout out of hearts and cling to the physical body like vine weeds. Weeds choke the life out of everything fruitful around them. Eventually a person's internal disposition begins to look like the yard of an abandoned house. Like an abandoned house, nothing can change until someone takes ownership. Since the abandoned house is you, you are the rightful person to assume ownership so that you can heal.

OWNERSHIP

Ownership is really the foundation for overcoming. Ownership is the right of all of Abba's sons and daughters. In fact, ownership is proof that you belong to Him and are no longer a slave. Because we are co-rulers with Him, we share in his possessions in the Earth. You are a part of his possession and He is your Lord. He is no slum Lord and takes care of all that belongs to Him. He has given you authority to obtain your healing. Right now you may look like an abandoned house. However, it is Abba's earnest desire and plans to rehabilitate you. You see, only slaves continue to reside in unkempt and unlivable conditions. Slaves don't have rights to own things—not even their own pain. They cannot afford to. The work to repair what is broken is too expensive, so they take whatever is given to them. Someone else will always be responsible for how they feel, what they think, what they like, what they don't like, and overall how they function. Abba's children, though, have the power to own and therefore overcome. In order to overcome something, you must have power and control over it. You must have permission to make executive decisions. This is why ownership is important. Jesus went to war to get the keys for dominion in the Earth back for us. We have to tap into that—especially when it comes to the conditions of our soul. We exercise this easily when it comes to stimulating our imagination through creativity, feeding our intelligence through learning new information, and disciplining our will by daily habits. Then there is the emotional center of the soul that we completely leave to its own free reign. We do very little to develop emotional maturity, emotional intelligence, and/or emotional fortitude. Most people have no contingency plan in place to recover from emotional trauma and turmoil and so things get completely out of control. We have to take control and own our emotional self.

RESPONSIBILTY, NOT FAULT

It's important to know that taking control and ownership of your pain is not the same as taking fault for it. I'm not suggesting that your pain is your fault, but it should become your responsibility. Much of the things that are going on in your soul are a result of things you've experienced at the hand people you loved and trusted. Everyone on planet earth that makes it pass the weaning age will experience emotional hurt of some kind. Some of it may be trivial and some of it may be extremely traumatic. The people who caused it, in most cases are not coming back to fix what they did. Even if they try to do it much later, you don't have the years to spend waiting. You probably have or had no control of what happened to you, but now you have the opportunity to control how you will recover. You have a choice on how your life will be and what kind of person you can become as a healed heart. You have to confront the totality of your story and really understand the role of all of the main characters. You have to be able to identify the villains and heroes throughout your life. You need to be able to identify the original seed of those vine weeds. You need to find the exact locations of where the roots begin to sprout out of the heart. This is important because you have to address emotional pain at the root or you will be cutting in futility. This is the full picture of what ownership looks like as it pertains to the soul.

RED TAPE | INTIMIDATION

If I am honest, I know that there is red tape that comes with taking ownership in all things. Ownership of your pain is not absent that red tape. Red tape represents the hindrances that keep us from fully being able confront everything that causes pain in our souls. There can be many things that simulate red tape when it comes to healing the soul. The first thing is often **intimidation.** As I said earlier, ownership requires you to confront and deal with the villains in your story. Most times the villains are people that you've loved and are close friends or family. That proximity always creates problems. Friends or former friend wounds are difficult to navigate but nothing beats the pain inflicted by family. Taking ownership of pain that comes from a family member can have some serious red tape in the form of intimidation due to family culture. Most families survive in dysfunction. The dysfunction is often trans-generational. The coping mechanism that the family adapts to is avoidance and silence. The thought is, if it's not acknowledged then it's not reality. It is the way of slaves and anyone that dares to break this mode of operation is a threat to the family secret. That person is at risk of being treated as an outcast or even as an enemy. In order to keep you in the way of the family, a strong wave of intimidation is used to keep you from speaking up. It is often projected from the elders of the family. They want to maintain a false sense of normalcy in the family dysfunction. They want this to remain uninterrupted and as quietly damming as possible. The truth is you may find that the offender is a repeat offender in the family. As you make strides to freedom, you will be made to feel like you are a villain in your attempt to be hero to yourself. They will often make you feel like something is wrong with you for seeking help outside of the family. There is an unwritten cultural rule among certain people groups that states, "What happens in [our] house stays [our] house." If you have heard this in your family, you are certainly under that intimidation *red tape*. This kind of oppressed thinking multiplies victims in the family and protects the victimizers. Please hear me! You have the right to own your pain and apprehend your healing no matter who doesn't like it. You are not obligated to keep the family secret and stay in bondage. Jesus did not die for us to remain captive as slaves, but he fought, bled, died, and resurrected so that we could obtain freedom through healing and deliverance. Although it may be taboo among your people to seek professional help, you don't have to ascribe to that bondage anymore. You have permission to apprehend your healing with all of your might. Let nothing stop you from owning your pain. Oh let me not forget to mention, the intimidation can come from other places. The person that caused the pain could be intimidating you. They probably started intimidating you at a young age to keep their secret. They may have told you a lie or threatened you so that you wouldn't tell your truth and expose them. They programmed you to fear an unlikely outcome. For years you may have bought into that tactic. I declare that today you can break free from that lie in your mind. The worse has already happened to you and now you need to see what its like to be free. One additional place that the intimidation may also come from is another victim in the family. They may not be ready to confront their pain. They are still governed by fear. The truth coming out will make them feel exposed and so they put pressure on you to not talk about it. They may or may not disclose that they are also a victim but will have a vested interest in your silence. You cannot let their fear and indecision keep you in bondage. You have the right to ownership. You are a son of God. You have the right to be free. Break the red tape.

RED TAPE | SHAME

The irritating thing about red tape is that it often has multiple layers. It is called red tape because it is very difficult to get through. It is designed to halt you in your mental progress. Another form of red tape in this pursuit of ownership of pain is most often **shame**. When you are victimized, you are often made to feel shame. Your feelings of shame guarantee the protection of the victimizer. Shame does a good job muzzling you. Shame steals your voice. It keeps you in a place where you feel like the pain inflicted upon you is your fault. If shame isn't projected on you, it can come through you. Depending on the infraction, you can feel extreme humiliation. You begin to recount your decisions and look for ways to write yourself in as the responsible party for your pain. Also, many times people turn to low places to numb the pain of the past. The things done in that state can bring shame and embarrassment that keep you from being able to address root issues. In some instances, you may have made missteps that led to the ultimate issue but you cannot allow shame to keep you from getting to your healing place. You can't allow shame to keep you in slavery. You can't allow shame to make you forfeit your rights of ownership and freedom as a son of God! Break the power of shame. Do what you need to do in the face of shame and burst through that red tape.

RED TAPE | PRIDE

This red tape is pesky and requires a quite a bit of work to press through, but its all worth it in the end. Ask anyone who has ever purchased a home. The freedom that comes with ownership is worth every battle that has to be fought on the upward climb. It is no difference when it comes to your soul being made whole. Of all the red tape, pride is the stickiest. Let me clarify! I don't mean haughtiness. I am talking about false humility. This kind of pride keeps a person thinking they are not even worth what Jesus paid and therefore they don't deserve to apprehend what he has offered. They don't believe they should ever have anything good. They often think they deserve whatever negativity comes their way. They live in a bubble of persistent condemnation and a false identity that keeps them from really seeing themselves as a son of God. Slavery is so normal, that they cannot fathom owning anything, especially their emotional well-being. When something good comes their way, they reject it, second guess it, or sabotage it through self-fulfilling prophecy. This kind of red tape is the most difficult because it is not imposed from the outside. Although it may have come from something that was spoken into the heart, it is self-inflicted. This may be your red tape. It is no one more difficult to be delivered from than self. If you are the source of your own chains, you have to fight and wrestle with your own mind to even begin to get free. When this form of a pride is at work, bondage and hurt are necessary environments to be maintained in order to perpetuate the narrative. You know this is red tape that you are dealing with when the door is open for freedom and you do not have the wherewithal to get up and walk through it.

The bottom line to all of the red tape is fear in one form or another. Fear causes paralysis to the soul. This fear will manifest in the body. The reason red tape exists in the world is fear and control based out of fear. It is no different when it comes to the immaterial part of who you are. Anybody that ever wanted to break through red tape to access anything had to have the tenacity, persistence, and resilience to keep going. I am telling you that your freedom and emotional wholeness are worth your effort. You can crush the lies of false humility by letting Abba speak to you about who you are from His point of view. You have to apprehend your healing. Jesus gave up his life convinced that you were entitled to freedom and absolutely worth it.

DON'T FEAR THEIR FACES

Throughout your journey to healing, you will have to have hard conversations. In some instances, you will have to confront people and the problems they bring that caused your hurt. Having said that, I am telling you to not be afraid of their faces. Abba will make your heart courageous if you trust Him to guide your process. Some of these experiences may not even be as hard as you think. Your honest communication with some people will bring liberty and change for you and them.

I personally recall having a difficult conversation with my mother. I honored her in the conversation, but I was honest about how some things in our relationship over the years negatively impacted my emotional health and development. I admit that I was very nervous to do this. I did not think that she would be as receptive as she was. I only knew that Abba said I needed to do this. So as I set there and unraveled 30 years of life in practically a 2-hour conversation, I watched how my mom was softened by my truth. Honestly, she never even would have thought about my point of view or how I was experiencing life with her if I did not say anything. She was accustomed to my adaptability. I was considered "emotionally strong". She knew that I had a tight relationship with God and therefore believed that I was ok without much input from her. In that conversation, we were both able to be immersed in the healing waters of God and repair many of the fractured parts of our relationship. It felt like we both learned the other person for the first time in that moment. God reintroduced and reacquainted us while giving us a completely new bond. Accountability was taken and apologies were rendered. This was an outcome that I did not know to plan for. I simply was obedient to Abba's leading. Now, I believe its is imperative to find the right timing and ensure that you are not still at the explosive anger phase of your hurt. You can pretty much bet that there will be no productive result to such kinds of conversations and confrontations. The person will immediately become defensive. Not simply because they don't want to take responsibility for what they have done, but, they will feel attacked. Our natural human response to being approached aggressively is to shift to a defensive posture. It is wise to allow yourself to be clear and sound with the ability to articulate your grievances with some substance and self-control. You should be resolved that not all of these conversations will end with apologies or the taking of responsibility. Your goal should be to take ownership of your pain. These conversations are meant to bring clarity and establish and reestablish boundaries that allow you to remain whole. Some of the conversations will be in parts. The initial part may not go well because the other party may need time with what you choose to share. It is most often true, if they are a person that brought hurt and pain to you, they too are suffering from hurt and pain of their own. It is probably true that their personal issues have not been resolved. Nor have they developed the skills to take personal accountability for the hurt they have caused. As the saying goes, "HURT PEOPLE, HURT PEOPLE!"

I recall having a challenging conversation with my father. I will admit the conversation was not as planned out and thorough as the one with my mother. We had had years of fragmented and inconsistent communication. I needed him to understand how his absence and lack of follow through had and was impacting me at the time. A presenting issue that was current provoked the conversation. My tenor was definitely a bit more sensitive. I was not exactly explosive, but I was matter of fact. This was a tone my father hadn't really heard from me. Here I am, his grown adult daughter confronting him for his behaviors. He was not yet ready to hear what I was saying. I can't say that I gave him much preparation. His initial response was to be very defensive. He employed whatever verbal warfare tactics he deemed necessary and relationship-appropriate to disarm my voice. My voice was a grenade that completely pearl harbored his life in that moment. He needed it to stop. As I said though, I know Abba was leading me to do the needful things to own my pain and begin to properly heal. Because I knew that, I did not withhold the truth. No matter the discomfort he felt, I still had to be accountable for myself. I honored him, but I was honest. He exited the conversation with my truth—no matter what. I was clear about what my objective was. Even if he did not want to accept what I was saying, I did it. In this instance, it was not a storybook ending. But some books end with cliffhangers until the sequel comes out. This conversation had a sequel. A few months later, I received a very heart-felt message from my father. He was honest about how my truth impacted him and where he was on the day that I shared it. After having some time with it, he was able to take personal responsibility for his contribution to my hurt and pain. We were able to come up with a resolve that would clear the path for Abba's healing waters to wash over and do the work for me and for him. There was no perfect thing to happen here. However, it gave an opportunity for growth.

FREEDOM IS THE DESTINATION

You have to be willing to do this work and not allow fear to keep you from doing it. No matter how vile and mean you believe your offender may be, if Abba leads you to have these exchanges, there is something you stand to gain. The only thing is, you cannot worry about trying to control what you gain. Abba has the thousand-foot view of your life and destiny. He knows what you need in order to become everything he intended. The truth is that freedom is the most important goal. If these confrontations and exchanges are ordered by heaven, they will lead to some version of freedom. It will all be a step toward ownership. Trust his leading. Allow freedom to come to you. Do what is needed to own your pain. You are becoming more and more unhindered to take your journey to the river.

Journey Thoughts | Chapter 5

1. Do you remember when the weeds were planted in your heart?
2. How do you feel about taking ownership of your pain?
3. Do you currently behave like an emotional slave? Are other people responsible for your mood and thoughts in a given day?
4. Have you considered a plan to improve your emotional health and intelligence?
5. Are you ready to take responsibility for your inner healing?
6. Do you feel intimidated by others to stay in your condition?
7. What part does shame play in your current emotional state?
8. Do you believe that you deserve to be whole?
9. What are some of the hard conversations that you may have to have on this journey?
10. What are some tools you can use to help you focus on freedom as you navigate the red tape?

JOURNEY TO THE RIVER

Chapter 6 – The Power of Full Disclosure

NEW PATIENT PAPERWORK

I would like for us to dive a bit more into the experience of moving toward the healing waters. I know we have spent some time talking about symptoms and even the self-medicating that we do in our journey. I want to move toward the part where we all should end up—purposefully and intentionally engaging God to pull us out of those patterns. I want to use the experience of the new patient at a doctor's office to convey some wisdom. I find it easy to talk about the healing of the soul by comparing it to the process that we go through when healing the physical body. There are many simple and powerful parallels. There is a great deal of wisdom to extract. The Holy Spirit used this experience to teach me valuable lessons about healing.

When a new patient enters into a doctor's office, they are required to go through a process. Oddly enough, as a person with a prescheduled appointment, you are one hundred percent more likely to do this. This isn't the case for emergency care services. This process occurs before the patient can actually meet with the doctor. The patient walks in and goes to the area assigned for check in. Once the receptionist verifies the identity and the appointment time, she asks if the patient is new. Then she reaches over to hand over the *dreadful* new patient paperwork. It can be such an inconvenience to have to fill out this extremely long document, but it is essential to whatever treatment or healing plan you will be prescribed by the doctor. Emergency care doesn't require this because the doctors there are only responsible for stabilizing you. They are not going to attend to a thorough overhaul. That's what specialist and primary care physicians are for. (This is why we have to stop only addressing the conditions of our souls with emergency care. We have to stop waiting until we are in a moment of full breakdown. It never leads to the full restoration that we need because we only focus on becoming stable in those times. The goal is to become whole again.)

The paperwork that a new patient has to fill out, helps create a very detailed picture that tells a doctor *who, what, when, where, and how* concerning the current condition that you are in. In a previous chapter, I told you that symptoms are powerful revelators and communicators. I meant that and I still holdfast to that. However, symptoms are not the only information to be gathered to begin your healing process. Without the other essential information components that you get from the new patient packet, there are a lot of wide holes in the picture needed for a more efficient healing process. The areas that are covered in the documentation are details I find just as essential to cover when dealing with the health of your soul. The four areas that new patient paperwork asks you for full disclosure about includes: **your history, your habits, your hosting & your happenings (or H4)**. There is extreme power and productivity in full disclosure. Honestly without it, I don't believe anyone is qualified to start the healing process completely. In your process you may not be required to gather this information for a third party, but it is essential for your personal journey. Let's spend some time talking about the significance of "H4" and the demand for full disclosure as you prepare for healing.

HISTORY

When it comes to healing, your history is very essential. In the case of physical health, the form asks you very intimate details. They ask you, in detail, about your family history. It is specific in asking about the medical conditions and diseases that your parents, grandparents, siblings, or children have had or are currently managing. The form asks cause of death if they have passed away. You also have to include any pre-existing medical conditions that you know about. You have to give account for any operations and serious injuries. If you are a woman, they want to know about your last menstrual cycle, pregnancies, live births, abortions or if you have experienced menopause. If you are a man, they want to know if you have had a vasectomy. Wow! This is an intense set of questions and it's not even all of them. But ask yourself, why are these things significant to disclose during this time?

Your history can often give insight to your wiring and explanation to your current state. The doctor is using this information to find the pathology of your condition. The same is true when dealing with the soul or emotional health. Understanding the storylines (in a basic way, at least) of all of the people directly connected to your storyline gives a better picture. This information offers deeper and a more accurate perspective. Perspective and clarity is very vital if you want to heal right. We have to be real about and aware of ourselves if we are serious about this journey. You have to know that pain takes away sensibility. In pain, we all tend to isolate our experiences and dehumanize the supporting cast in our thriller-saga. Unprocessed pain has a way of emptying us of healthy amounts of empathy and fueling us with anger and judgment. We are hardly rational enough to see the trees for the forest. Although it may be fueled by fear or self-preservation, our world becomes extremely small with no space for complete pictures about those who may have intentionally or unintentionally contributed to our soul's condition.

Let me be personal for a minute. In my journey, I could not even begin to fully deal with the trauma of my childhood and the disappointments that I felt until I gave my parents permission to be people first. In doing that, I recounted their stories and what happened or didn't happen in their upbringing. Recounting this history gave me a chance to realize that they too had traumas that they did not have time to address or recover from before they had children. So now you have two traumatized individuals coming together to attempt to care for a soul without any real tools. Hear me! I didn't remove the responsibility from them to be accountable for things that were done or not done; but I was also able to have some compassion for them and forgiveness toward them. This opened up a channel for more effective communication between them and I. Being able to dial into history can give you that gift.

History also helps you understand the source of some of your proclivities and preferences. You need to know what kinds of things were wrestled with before you came on the scene or earlier in your life. Every battle your predecessors faced and didn't overcome, you will eventually have to deal with. (The same is true for you and the generation that comes from you.) You will find that you were predisposed for a lot of the things that you have experienced. Having an awareness of your history gives you fighting and healing knowledge. Knowing your history can help you learn what you have the potential to produce or become in a negative and positive sense. You have to be reminded of the things that came out of you at different seasons. It also lets you know what you cannot bring forth. History helps build context around pains and hurts. You need context or your actual identification of the root issue can lack accuracy or take a longer time to be determined. This, in turn, holds up the forward movement in your healing journey. Looking at all of this information collectively is a wild experience but you will feel connected in a way that you never have. Your understanding will be opened in new ways. History isn't meant to give you excuses but it does point to explanations for certain things. You need to know this in order to start healing.

HABITS

History is for context, but once you are placed in a context, it's time to find the dysfunctional and unfruitful patterns in your life. This is the next area that you have to give full disclosure for. In a new patient packet, this is the section where you explore your habits. Within the medical arena, they ask about your patterns in direct ways. You will see questions like the following: Do you smoke? Do you drink? Frequency? Sexual Activity? Menstrual Cycle Regularity? What is your fitness level or lifestyle? What is the average number of hours you sleep daily? It is important to learn these things because you can learn what things are negatively impacting your health or you can see habits (or the lack there of) that arise as a response to the current condition of your health. Your doctor will see these things and ask you questions based upon what they believe needs more clarity to make connections.

Identifying patterns of brokenness is also paramount as it pertains to the healing journey. Some behavior patterns you have developed can be an offshoot of the underlying soul issue and others are developed as coping mechanisms. (For example, you do not like expressing your feelings face to face with people so you avoid sensitive dialogue. You will only share what you *feel* via text message. You do this because as a child in your household you were never given an opportunity to express any emotion. You were even hit for crying or getting upset for things that should be deemed appropriate.)

Some habits may not all be unhealthy, bad, or evil but may be motivated by hurt. Any habit that you create in brokenness is often out of balance. You can do good things with the wrong motivation. If you could not produce the same consistency in a healthy space, it is worth evaluating. (For example, you are extremely health conscious because growing up you were belittled or made fun of for being heavy. Now you workout beyond the recommended amount for your frame and eating unusually low amounts of calories out of fear of gaining weight.) Frequency and intensity of behaviors are important to take note of for this very reason.

Your habits can tell you a lot about the condition of your soul. It is important to allow God to take you on the journey of "WHY?" You need to understand the motivation behind the things you do. The opposite is also true. There may be good habits that you have a hard time keeping. For example, why aren't you resting and going to bed? Why can you never keep appointments? Why can't you eat according to your diet—what's your connection to food? The inability to be consistent with habits can give you a lot of insight about the condition of your soul also. If you are willing to dig in for the answers, the river is closer than you think.

HOSTINGS

As you move onward as *new patients,* the paperwork will ask you about your hosting. A better way to say hosting is *environment*. History forms context, habits identifies themes, and hosting gives you setting. The physician can tell you a lot about your condition if he knows where you have been and/or who has been around you. They often ask you if you have traveled out of the country and if you have, they want to know where. Some of them ask if you have hosted a person from another nation in your home. The reason for this information is 3-fold. Our nation has a medical system that integrates vaccinations to its citizens so certain diseases are pretty much done away with in our region. However, if you have traveled abroad, you may have reintroduce risks of exposure that you otherwise would not have. Also, some diseases are prevalent in specific regions and nations. Medical practitioners have that information in a database and by having it they are allowed to broaden the scope of their diagnostic testing when they are aware. Lastly, it's easy to narrow down a source or host of specific sickness if there is a subject that is not a constant inserted into the study. Who you host can have impact on what you are exposed to. Now, this is just looking at it from the medical viewpoint.

As you manage looking into your soul health, being aware of where you have been and who you have been around throughout the years can be very pivotal pieces to the puzzle. Our souls are sticky and pick up a lot of stuff from the traffic of our lives. There are some things in your heart that are not necessarily *yours* but you picked it up from engaging with specific individuals. Soul ties are real. I don't know if you have ever noticed yourself picking of character traits of people you have spent intimate time with or share close proximity with. It is not always bad but it's also not always good. Sometimes you can pick up moods and demeanors. You know you have been in a room and its normal and easy and then a new person enters and the whole atmosphere of the room goes down. In individual moments like that, your soul may not be impacted long term but if you are constantly engaging and exchanging with a person who is always depressed or sad, eventually that will become your mood too. You find yourself feeling heavy too.

Environments matter, period. What you can't find in your history or habits can mostly like be found in the hosting. You may find that a lot of the reason you are the way you are is because of the environments you were raised in. It is not just people and things that are outwardly shown by them. A person raise in a neighborhood that was known for violence and hostility can have a major impact. You may not specifically have had a reason to be violent or angry but somehow you still seemed to have become volatile and eruptive for simple things in your adult life. Environments can create spiritual entanglement. We say people are *products of their environment* but no one has to remain in that state. As you move toward healing, you will find that environments will be brought up again and again. Environments can break you down but the environments you keep can also heal you and help you stay whole.

HAPPENINGS

Continuing with the new patient analogy, lastly, the areas that are typically covered are the happenings. These things are normally found out in the demographic section like your age, marital status, number and age of children, occupation, or other things that would impact or be included in your day-to-day functioning. These things are good to be disclosed because they can often contribute to the current condition you have to manage.

In matters of the heart, happenings are equally telling. Happenings add texture and development to the overall story that you need to be able to see concerning yourself. Happenings include the responsibilities, roles, and relationships of your life. If you already have an underlying root issue, sometimes your day-to-day responsibilities and relationships can amplify, magnify or intensify the problem when it goes unaddressed. Sometimes these things add pressure onto already sensitive areas. For example: you may have had absentee issues with your father and now you are newly married. You find it hard to trust the words of your husband and often find it difficult to allow his input in matters of household leadership. This has become a strain to you as a newly wed. As you prepare for healing, you will have to allow God to show what things are being affected by your brokenness because once you are healed; you will have to reconcile these areas too. It is of high value that you really pay attention to the things that are going on right in front of you everyday so that you can get further along in your journey toward healing.

FULLY DISCLOSED

This "H4" process requires a lot investigation, introspection, and honesty, but it is all very needful. As I said earlier, this sharing may be between you and God (or maybe someone he appoints to walk with you through this) but really this ultimately is to help you see yourself clearly. It is not until you can come completely face-to-face with a clear picture of yourself that you are ready to immerse into the healing waters of God. This is why you have to go through this process to develop a complete story. The more information you can fill in during this process, the better the prognosis for wholeness. Full disclosure and complete honesty with **yourself** is required of you so that you can become unhindered to heal. You can do this! I am rooting for your soul to become whole.

Journey Thoughts | Chapter 6

1. As you prepare for this journey how does the requirement of full disclosure make you feel?
2. What do you look forward to learning from digging into history and the stories tied to yours?
3. Have you ever investigated these things before? What was the outcome then?
4. Are you willing to be completely honest about your habits? Does looking at your habits make you feel embarrassed?
5. Do you remember a lot about the environment that you were raised in? (Neighborhood, family culture, spiritual climate)
6. Do you understand its impact on who you have become today?
7. Who has come into your life and had the greatest and worse possible impact on your character and emotional health? Why?
8. When you look at your life today, what are some of the current happenings that are a result of your current emotional state or historical trauma? (Job, Spouse, Parenting style, etc.)
9. As you have explored these areas, what has been your most insightful finding about yourself?

Part 3
Wisdom for the Stay

JOURNEY TO THE RIVER

Chapter 7 – Sterile Healing Environments

ENVIROMENTS MATTER

Over the course of the last several chapters, I have pointed you to things that you should be aware of as you make your way toward healing. As you move forward in wisdom and insight, I want to now help you by preparing you for things that are universally helpful when healing. As I said, each person's treatment will be different but there are some things that are pretty normal in the preparation, process, and recovery.

In the previous chapter, I told you that the importance of environments would come up again and again. Just as environments can help break you down, they also can incubate you for healing and help you maintain your wholeness. As you prepare to go into one of the most sensitive times of your life, you will need to be in sterile healing environments. I extracted this wisdom from a very practical place. I thought about the level of care you get when in a medical facility during surgery and recovery. Even if you have never had surgery or had to be hospitalized for severe issues, you've at least had a relative or friend in this situation. There is one thing that is constant during times like this: a lot of focus put on the environment.

VULNERABILITY

Last chapter we discussed full disclosure, which is a deep level of vulnerability. That is a preparatory step, but once you actually spend time with God and those he appoints, your soul healing procedure will be performed. There may have to be removal of things from the heart. There may be a need to stitch open wounds. Some wounds will have to be reopened and cleaned out. No matter the procedure, all of it leaves you very vulnerable. When you are vulnerable at this magnitude, you are susceptible to anything. You are at risk of pouring out too much. You are at risk of contamination. You are extremely fragile. You can potentially lack judgment and accuracy in discernment. Your vision will most likely not be clear. There will be pain that has to be managed. So much about your forward progress is at stake and that is the reason why you have to be cautious about your environment.

EXPOSURE

Much of a hospital's concern for environment and its sterility has to due with preventing exposure. Healing is a process that needs to be done behind closed doors. Have you ever seen a doctor perform a surgery on the street? Have you ever seen someone dealing with their surgery wounds publicly? I certainly hope not. That person would be in danger of all kinds of bacteria infections. That doctor would be at risk of malpractice and lawsuits. Your soul (well, your heart) is a very a sensitive part of you and should be handled with gloved hands in sterile environments.

If you mismanage your environments during times of healing, you potentially heal wrong or make the condition worse than it was before touching it. There are people who have gone in for surgeries that are fairly easy to manage by any trained doctor. However, during recovery, the environment was not sterile as needed (or something was introduced into the environment accidentally) and some ended up needing another procedure and others died because of exposure. Now I am not suggesting literal death in matters of emotional health, but aborting destiny and purpose can be the outcome and is equivalent to death in this case.

To limit exposure, most hospitals limit who you can come in contact with during this time. People can love you and mean well but still have limited to no access to you for a time. There are people who are close to you but their proximity during times of healing can be contaminating. (For example: During your healing time, you could be releasing forgiveness for a third party who violated you. If a person close to you has an offense with that third party or had a recent confrontation with them and comes to you to vent at this sensitive time, it could completely set you back in your process. In extreme circumstances, it may make it difficult to forgive them at all.) It is important to be vigilant about the sterility of your environment when you are trying to heal. Don't let people close to you talk you into overexposure. Do not succumb to the pressure of trying to *normalize* yourself during this season. It is perfectly ok for you to take a timeout and communicate as much to your community of family and friends. Limit exposure as much as possible to reduce the chance for *infection* to enter into your soul.

EXPERTS

In fact, in the most vulnerable stages, you should only be allowing experts to aid in the healing process. I am advocating for therapy and counseling. I am not eliminating people outside of that field by saying experts. I am simply saying this isn't the time for simple "girl talk" or " guy talk". You need to be interacting with people of wisdom and objectivity. Let these people have command of their own lives. It is unwise to heal with a bleeding friend. I'm not saying that God can't sovereignly use anyone, but that is not wise or practical. I would say, that is for downright emergencies only. For this scenario, we are talking about thorough processes that lead to healing the soul completely. You also do not want to engage people who are *too close* to the issues of your heart. Some of your loved ones are protectors and defenders by nature. You share your wounds with them and they are ready to go to war. They will further incite you or you will have to expend your energy trying to bring them back down at a time that you are trying to find peace and wholeness for yourself.

There is a reason why during the most vulnerable times in a medical facility, the patient only interacts with the staff assign to their case. Another piece of wisdom to be extracted here is: specify your experts. There maybe a few different people in your life that you feel could potentially help you through this process. There may be people who think that because they went through trauma, they have the know how to manage your soul. Pray and use wisdom. There are several doctors in a hospital, but the one that attends to the patient in surgery is a specialist according to the condition that is being addressed. Even in that, there maybe more than one specialist in that specialty but only one is assigned to lead the case. This keeps confusion down. Each expert has their own approach to fixing problems. They may confer, but ultimately a choice has to be made by the person leading the case. You don't want too many voices, too much advice, or too many directions being given to you at once. You want to simplify your process. This also still impacts the sterility of your healing environment.

INTENSIVE CARE

There is another component to be mindful of as it pertains to environments. When a patient is going through the preparing, procedure, and recovery of surgery, they also have levels of care. The levels of care indicate the intensity of sterility, the specification for boundaries, and the limitation in activity. The most vulnerable and extreme cases are placed in intensive care. In intensive care, a patient is at their weakest and at the highest levels of risk. Sometimes they are classified as *critical condition*. (A heart full of pain is always a critical condition.) Patients in intensive care are extremely limited in interaction. Even the expert personnel have to take extreme precautionary measures to ensure sterility because of the level of sensitivity. Most often, (if anyone) only the closest next of kin is allowed in close proximity. That is often within a certain time frame and most often with supervision. We have to be just as considerate when it comes to healing soul wounds. It is very important that you are mindful about boundaries. Yes, this may be hard for you to establish or challenging for your love ones to receive but it is for everyone's best interest. The people or person that may be aiding you also will have to be mindful of how they approach you and communicate with you. A fragile heart can't take much. You should also be reducing your extracurricular activities to a bare minimum. In fact, this time should include only the roles, responsibilities, and routines that are absolutely necessary. Remember this will be during the most critical time of healing.

REGULAR CARE

After a patient has crossed over the most challenging thresholds of risk during recovery, they are normally transferred to the traditional recovery suite. It is important to note that this patient is still in the care of and under the charge of the surgeon and his or her support staff. Although, the most sensitive time has been endured, very intentional care and monitoring is still required. Also, within the recovery suite, sterility is still a priority. The patient can interact with a few more visitors but still not an entire community of people. Most hospitals set limits for the number of people that can be in the room at a time. They will also enforce visiting hours because during recovery, rest is highly important. Introducing stress can impact the oxygen and blood flow and severely decrease the pace of healing.

When you are going through your healing process, don't get too lackadaisical concerning boundaries and environment because you feel like you are out of the darkest spot. All of it takes is for one careless act and a wound could be reopened before the healing could fully take place. You may be thinking I am being too specific but I've seen what an unprocessed comment has done to a tender heart. If you are honest with yourself, you know you don't want to even run that risk because you know how you can be. Keep in mind that in this state, any movement and activity is assisted and only for the benefit of the healing process. You are not in the position to help anyone else. I know some of you are so used to helping everyone else that you feel strange when you have sit still for a while. RESIST THE URGE, PLEASE.

HOME & FOLLOW-UP CARE

The patient will get to a stage of progress in healing that does not require around-the-clock care or monitoring. During this time, they are released to go home, but they are given detailed instructions for home maintenance and follow-up care. Most of the time that instruction includes steps to keep the surgical site clean, rest, activity limitations, and a schedule for follow-up appointments. Interacting with people isn't as highly guarded and sterility can be mildly managed.

For matters of the heart, this means that you can slowly start introducing people back into your space but be mindful about who can get extremely close. The person that is aiding you will start giving you a little space. The most important thing to adhere to at this time is rest. You will need to learn to just spend time with God alone so that he can begin to pour back into you. There is a time when you need intense support but now you will need to fully give your attention back to God so that he can build your strength. Don't make an idol out of the support system. They are an extension of God's compassion but they did not replace God. Be mindful not to guilt them into maintaining the same intensity and availability to prove their love to you. You will be fine with God. I'm not saying they completely drop you off here. Their presence and voice will reduce in intensity every time you move in your levels of care toward full recovery.

Also, don't get back into old patterns because you are in a comfortable space. Sometimes when a patient gets home from surgery, they start trying to resume their life as usual. Accept that you are not yet ready to do everything. Again, I should emphasize that resting is important. Physical rest is a necessity, but so is emotional and mental rest. Many times people end up in horrible conditions simply because they choose not to rest. They choose not to just spend time with God allowing him to finish bringing them to full strength or rejuvenation. Interestingly enough, in the natural course of things, this stage is typically the longest. (I think God has a sense of humor in doing this.) We often have the hardest time being still. Fight the urge to prove that you are ready to be back out on the scene. You aren't ready at this stage. I promise you it's better to wait until God says you are ready. If you do things prematurely, you can end up with an irreparable injury or handicap. The worse thing you can do is *bare down on a muscle* that's not yet ready to be used. The impact is horrible for you and potentially cataclysmic for the intended audience. All of us are due for a *cut* at some point in our journey and it's for our good. But none of us should handle people while we are still bleeding. It is a travesty to *bleed* on the people that we are supposed to help. (Notice I didn't say, "bleed for" because Jesus did that and that would be Christ-like.) I will say again, you must master rest during this time. If you can rest and follow God's prompts, you will make it to full recovery and be better than ever.

LIGHT DUTY

There is one final stage you want to keep in mind as it pertains to managing environments and sterility for healing and recovery. This stage is known as "light duty". When a recovering patient has transitioned to light duty, they can return to work and life duties but at a reduce pace and intensity. Of course, this is the least restrictive of all of the stages. Sterility is not really mentioned at all.

Gaining strength and mobility is of the greatest importance. Support at this time is so minimal that it can feel like your *experts* have jumped ship. However, in this stage, you are regaining your independence and stretching back out into your stride—little by little. There is only one precaution: don't overdue it. You are not quite 100%. Don't dive heart first into any new endeavor or relationship. Ease into your stride. This is the time where you reintroduce the things that you were restricted from in small doses.

Do not go full force until Abba gives you the release. You will personally know when its time. There is no residue from the pain that was once there. You won't be afraid to use your *range of motion*. You will be ready to thrust toward your destiny without hesitation or restraint from issues of the past.

MIND YOUR ENVIROMENTS

You are on this preemptive discourse now, but as you move forward toward your healing journey, sterile environments will be crucial. Your attentiveness to the boundaries at each stage is imperative. Maintaining low visibility and protecting high vulnerability is your pathway to success. Don't spend this time in worry over people who choose not to understand your needs in recovery. Enjoy your time in temporary obscurity. Be unhindered to heal. Take this time seriously and personally like your destiny and purpose depend on—well, because they do.

Journey Thoughts | Chapter 7

1. How do you normally behave when you feel vulnerable or exposed in an emotional way?
2. Do you recall a time where you might have been around the wrong places or people at a sensitive time? What came of that moment?
3. Have you identified or heard from God about who your qualified *experts* should be during this process? (A therapist, a mentor, a mature friend, spiritual leader?)
4. In the intensive care stage of healing, how will you create and communicate boundaries with your community?
5. In the home care stage of healing, what will resting look like for you?
6. How will you manage the change in dependency with your *experts*?
7. What are some safeguards that you can put in place ensure that you remain on light duty for the proper amount of time?
8. How important is the management of your environments while healing? Level of urgency as you prepare?

JOURNEY TO THE RIVER

Chapter 8 – *You Can Heal Wrong*

PEELING SCABS

Beautiful Soul! Thank you for continuing with me on this journey. You are doing great! I pray that you are allowing Abba's wisdom to break into the guarded areas of your heart. I pray that with every principle, you are becoming more prepared for the journey ahead. In an earlier chapter we delved into hindrances of time. There was one thing that I did not mention as it pertains to time. You may have had your condition for a while now. Your trauma and brokenness has probably been with you for a great many of years. In fact, any amount of years is longer than acceptable for any of Abba's sons and daughters. With the passing of time, we can often be deceived by false healing. A *scab* may have formed but the wound can have an infection in it. It can still be tender to touch. In some cases, if someone touched it, it provokes you to violence or breakdown. This *scab* is going to have to be removed and cleaned out. Abba is not interested in us *healing* like this. He is looking at your brokenness and saying, "I know you think this is healed, but you've healed wrong!" Instead of going the distance of the journey for complete healing, we tend to do our own rigging. We never get to truly fix the real issues but we do just enough to *make due*. This is not Abba's designation for us. I know this all too well.

LESSONS FROM THE BONES

When the Lord said this to me a few years ago, I was stunned—but I knew it was true. As hardened as I had become, under all of that, I still dealt with so many emotional differences. In that time, I was taken back to my childhood. As a child, I had a love for basketball. I always wanted to play on an organized team in the community or at school. Somehow, I was never able to coordinate with my mom to pay the physical fees on the day that the doctor would come to the school for all potential players. After a while, I just gave up. I still had an opportunity to connect to the court because in my community, street ball was always in order. Pick-up games happened all of the time. All of the athletes that were excelling on the organized teams would come play at the court in my neighborhood. Every now and then, I would get picked to play on their teams. You couldn't tell me I wasn't the next best thing touching a basketball. One day I shot a 3-Pointer while being pushed in the grass by a grown man and *it went INNNNN!* I was famous for a day. (Oh, my goodness! LOL!) I tell you these stories to allow you to see how close I was to the sport. While being at these games, people would get all kinds of injuries. People (girls and guys) were fouled hard often in street ball. This style of the game was more about grit than it was about basketball IQ. I've seen people with bloodied noses and lips keep playing and leaving proud with their injuries. The injury that I saw the most was finger jams and breaks. Catching a flaming basketball pass from an athlete, who regularly played quarterback on the football team, was always interesting. The adrenaline of the game almost always made people play on. I know on many occasions people would assume that they had a finger jam and keep playing. When it truly was a jam, over time, the finger would unlock and return to the regular functionality. Now, there were a few instances that players would actually have broken fingers. They would assume that it was a jam. They would continue to play. They would, at best, ice the finger and place a wrap on the hand and keep it moving. After a few weeks, the pain would be minimal and they would take the wrap off. The fingers would not look exactly the same. It would look slightly crooked and could not bend regularly anymore. After a short time, some of the athletes who were going on to play on a collegiate and, potentially, a professional level, would add some redress to correct the fingers. They would visit a doctor. The doctor would identify that the finger must have been broken at one time or another. The doctor would tell them, "You will be fine with the finger in its current condition. You will be able to do ok as it is. However, if you want the finger to have its highest functionality, we can reset it." At this point the athlete would decide if they wanted to endure the pain of having the bone reset or settle for minimal functionality with the finger. I knew both kinds of athletes. This part of my childhood taught me a great deal of wisdom as it pertains to healing and healing wrong.

UNDERESTIMATING THE IMPACT

The very first principle that I picked out from this story here is that, just like those athletes, many of us underestimate the impact of the initial pain. The athlete did not realize that they actually broke a bone because of the adrenaline of the game. Often times we are in the throws of life—simply surviving and we underestimate or under calculate the fall out of the initial blow that was handed to us. Words, absences, hits, and/or other egregious acts inflicted on us may have been just absorbed because of the speed of the life that we were accustomed to living. Just like those athletes, getting fouled hard was part of the culture of our lives and so we learned to suck up the pain and *play through it*—no matter how severe it was. The danger of underestimating the initial impact is that we begin fostering an environment where people regularly healed wrong.

In many cases, we do as the athletes do. We find our quick fix that does nothing to address the actual brokenness. It does just enough to comfort us while passing over the greatest thresholds of pain. All the while, we don't realize that the *bones are setting* in whatever way they are positioned. The body is intelligently designed in that way. It always tries to find a way to mend itself. It naturally wants things to come together. We see that from scars and wounds and even hair. Left unattended, the body will produce its on way. This is not different in the mental and emotional realm. Your whole person tries to heal itself. Just like the body, in order to heal properly, it needs to be guided.

STUNTED POTENTIAL

Without proper identification and guidance, the areas that are broken will begin to set and harden. Bones fuse back together, but hearts harden and mindsets crystalize. Many of us don't realize that most of our emotional wounds have hardened and have become a part of us. The awful truth is that pain will embed itself into your personality if not addressed. Much of who we become is a mutated version of the blueprint that God designed. We regularly normalize the dysfunction in our lives. It becomes a natural part of our everyday routine. Just like the crooked fingers of those athletes, many of our lives become warped versions of what they were supposed be. To be completely honest, most of us can make it out *o. k.* with this version of life. We aren't completely handicapped by the blows that we emotionally incurred. Certainly, our emotional flexibility and adaptability may be challenged to a degree, but we can be otherwise successful in life with a little effort. The truth is, Abba isn't ok with you living with stunted potential. He did not give his best for you to settle for the mediocre version of this life. He did not spend heaven's greatest resource for you to not fulfill your destiny. What's the point of living a decent life and not fulfill your destiny? Like those athletes, you can settle for the glory experienced *playing street ball* or you can prepare to move to the next level.

DIAGNOSIS & DECISIONS

This is the point at which you would expose yourself to a doctor. As I told you, the athletes that became more disciplined to prepare to move to the next level always begin to take care of their physical body on a more intensive level. They often saw sports medicine professionals. In that relationship, the doctor is always able to point out to the athlete the current condition and history of their body. In this case, the doctor could identify that the finger was once broken and healed wrong. As the doctor is to the athlete, so is Abba as it pertains to our souls. As we grow and mature and subject ourselves to his intimate observation, he will begin to show us things in us that were broken and healed wrong. God will begin to unpack your history by highlighting one "crooked finger" or mal-adjusted behavior. He starts showing us who we have currently become and how we got to be this way. He will identify why we respond to certain people, places, and things the way we do. Like any good doctor, Abba will present us with the option. We can do fine in life with our *crooked finger* or we can allow it to be reset. The choice is always ours.

TO RESET OR NOT TO RESET?

Abba absolutely wants us to be put into the best possible position to be whole—with nothing missing, nothing broken, and nothing lacking. However, He also honors our right to choose. The honest truth is: wrapping the heart and mind around being reset is a lot. You see, when the break happened in real time, the adrenaline of survival and shock absorbed the weight of it for the most part. To willingly sit and prepare for someone to purposefully crack into some part of you is a huge pill to swallow. Although the pain will lead to healing and restoration, it is still a major threshold that has to be crossed. It takes a lot of courage, emotional control, and mental focus to endure it. The first break you didn't have to decide on or brace for it. It seems as if pain that you have to anticipate seems worse. You mentally go through all of the worse case scenarios. This is why in situations like tooth pulling, shots, or any other pain-based actions that are done to us—the person doing the actions against us tries to create some element of surprise or distraction. When there is a resetting, there is no surprise or distraction. In fact, your full participation is required. You have to willingly yield to it's happening. Now the Chief Physician is standing before you asking, "Will you be reset?"

WILL YOU BE MADE WHOLE?

"Will you be reset?" is the same as asking "Will you be made whole?" You see, this question has a plethora of complexities. In fact, I know a biblical story that directly brings out the wisdom of this contemplation. In the fifth chapter of the book of John, Jesus goes to the Bethesda Pool in Jerusalem where there were many sick people. There was a man there who had a condition for thirty-eight years. The scripture says that Jesus knew he was there for a long time. It follows to say that Jesus asked him directly "Will you be made whole?" I find it interesting that this question did not have anything to do with this man's spiritual faith. This question was targeted to the soul of the man. In reality, this man was seated right by the healing waters. His journey to healing was not even afar off. He was so close to healing but his emotional and mental state did not allow for him to go get in. His heart and mind had crystalized where he just accepted his broken state—so much so, he was lame or immobile. The bible said he had an infirmity but never identified what it was. He had it so long that it brought him to a complete halt. Sure, he was alive. He was in a community of people. The scriptures say there were many lame people there. He was also able to witness the power of God. The scriptures say that he would literally witness the angel come down and stir up the healing waters repeatedly. Many of us look like this man in the Spirit Realm. We have created a functional version of our dysfunction. It is now that Jesus enters and asks the soul-permeating question, "Will you be made whole?" This is God asking to reset you in your heart and mind. This is God asking if he can disrupt the chaos. This is Him asking to unpack your thirty-eight years (or whatever the number is). This is Him saying to you "let me break your brokenness so that you can get up and walk."

I know that you have acclimated yourself to living comfortable (to the best of your ability) in your discomfort. Just like the man, you just need someone to intercede and step in the middle of your chaos and ask you an obvious question. Here he was lying there and watching other people get into that water. He was bothered by it, but he was lying with other sick and lame people. Who was he going to be able to express his frustration to? He was lying there while other people literally walked over him and received the thing that he always wanted—to be whole. When Jesus asked him, it caused that which was in his heart to come out. Not only did he have the infirmity, he also felt neglected and left alone. In one question, Jesus addressed his soul hurts and put the man in the position to apprehend his healing. This man was able to choose to be reset. He didn't even have to get into the water for it to happen. Much of his stagnation had to do with how his mind and heart had crystalized while sitting there waiting on someone else to give him what only he could chose for himself.

BREAKING THE BROKEN HEART

Abba's desire is to reset you so that you can get up and walk into your destiny. He has to confront your brokenness that crystalized and embedded into your person. Your heart has sustained many blows. In the fight to survive, it has fused back together. However, it has healed wrong. His goal is to break your broken heart. He breaks it to align it and mend it together. This is the season that you have to decide if you willing to acknowledge that you healed wrong. This is the day that you either will accept your condition and keep it or allow Abba to reset you. In your resetting, you may have to revisit some of the steps in the journey. It will only help you become whole. I beg of you to let him disrupt your chaos and call you on Journey to the River.

Journey Thoughts | Chapter 8

1. When you experienced trauma or pain, did you ever take a processing pause or did you just move with the pace of life at the time?
2. Have you ever considered the impact of those experiences?
3. What do you believe that experience has done in your heart? How has is shaped your worldview?
4. Considering hindsight, what growth or flourishing opportunities have you missed out on because of stunted potential?
5. Do you want to live out the rest of your days with the possibilities of missing out on new doors, relationships, and chances for growth?
6. How would you respond if you were told that you healed wrong?
7. What would be the greatest challenge to being reset for you? How would you overcome it?
8. Like the man at Bethesda, how has your mindset kept you from the healing waters?

JOURNEY TO THE RIVER

Chapter 9 – Sequential Effects of Healing

A WORD OF CAUTION

As with the last chapter, I want to extend wisdom for something you should prepare for as you approach your healing journey. We have already made it clear that healing is a complicated process and can be extremely uncomfortable for various reasons. However, I think it's one thing that you need to be prepared for or you will jump out of the water too soon. In fact, you may quit on your way to the water if you aren't given this information. It is imperative that you come to grips with the **sequential effects** of the healing process. All healing has sequential effects. Sequential effects are different from side effects.

SIDE EFFECTS vs. SEQUENTIAL EFFECTS

See, you are accustomed to hearing about side effects. When you are getting treatment for a medical condition, you are often prescribed a pharmaceutical drug. The drug may be used to address a condition in the body. However, the introduction of that synthetic material to the body causes new negative conditions that, in some cases, are worse than what you started with. For example, you can take a pill to treat a minor back pain but it could potentially cause dehydration, constipation, heart palpations, fever, and potentially death. This is the result of imperfect people attempting bring the body back to its perfect state with limited means. But what happens when God is doing the healing? What happens when he begins to heal the soul? This brings me, again, to sequential effects. Sequential Effects are the opposite of side effects. Side effects cause sicknesses to be more complex. Sequential effects cause healing to be a lot more complex. Let's explore the complexities for a better understanding.

For Starters, when God heals, it's on a dimensional level and not just on the surface. His healing can also be generational and environmental. When God begins to heal you in one area it will begin to ricochet into other areas within you and impact lives outside of yours. He moves throughout your inner man to find the fractures, holes, and contamination in your soul. He thoroughly investigates all of the root causes and makes judgments about how to bring healing. This reality contributes to the sequential effects of healing.

MISDIRECTION OF PAIN

Sequential effects encapsulate the management and mastery of the healing process. One sequential effect is managing the misdirection of pain. God addresses the misdirection of pain in our soul as a part of the process. Abba's response to our cry of pain gives great revelation of how this is handled. You may present Him with one thing to heal because that is the area that is of great concern to you. He *might* attend to that area, (maybe right then or later) but he often heals something that is of greater value or higher importance from His viewpoint. He has to bypass our experience with secondary pain in order to truly make us whole. Honestly, this proves how *good* he is. Let me tell you why. See, we don't really understand our pain enough to know how it needs to be healed. In the medical field, there is something called secondary hyperaglesia. In plain language, it's when you have a higher sensitivity to pain in an area of your body as a result of an injury—but outside of the injury site due to a malfunction in the nervous system. (For example: you injure your hand at work pretty badly but for some reason your forearm –that wasn't injured—is signaling a higher amount of pain.) This can be pretty common in the physical body. We, too, can experience a version of *secondary hyperaglesia* on an emotional and mental level when we endure trauma and dysfunction.

God has the ability to see beyond our cries. When we need healing, we point God to the area that really wasn't the primary injury because our ability to distinguish pain has been impaired. So, as I said, God may address the pain that we point him to, but often times he goes to the injury site or the root issue first. Then he begins to rewire our sensory organ—thusly, making the healing process have sequential effects.

There is a biblical story that comes to mind that illustrates the Lord doing this. In the fourth chapter of the book of John, Jesus has an encounter with a woman at the well. They start having a conversation about water and the history of the well. On a deeper level it was a conversation about her inability to worship God. Her soul was missing worship. She felt like the chief problem that kept her from true worship was culture. This woman was at a watering (or healing) place as you are planning to go. She presented her grievances to the Lord and he seemingly flipped the script. Jesus says to her in the middle of the conversation, "Go, call your husband and come back." The scripture says that the woman had no husband. She had been with several men and currently in an intimate relationship with a man who was also not her husband. Now this address seems to not have a context to her initial grievance of broken worship, but Jesus wanted deal with the actual root issue that caused her hurt in the first place. Her chief complaint was culture, but her real problem was intimacy. Jesus showed her this by touching the other broken patterns of relationships in her life. He is such a great healer. He can discern the misdirection of our pain and heal root causes. Enduring the process of that is a whole other animal.

INCREASE IN PAIN

Sequential effects categorize a multitude of things that happen within the healing process. Another sequential effect is gaining tolerance for the pain that is incurred in the application of various treatment types. We know the pain that we are accustomed to carrying with our traumatic history. What we don't know is the pain that is to be expected from treatment. As I said, the Lord walks throughout your inner man locating fractures, breaks, holes, and contamination in our souls. Each of those things requires different treatment modalities.

For fractures and breaks, setting and casting is required to ensure proper alignment when restored. *Setting* requires the further breaking and maneuvering of something that is normally supposed to be immovable, thereby causing pain. Casting causes restriction and lost of mobility. If you have ever known anyone with a cast, you have seen the torture of having an itching place that can't be reached for scratching and relief.

For holes, you will need stitches to seal them up. Stitches are disruptive because it is the intentional and continuous piercing of a sensitive area in a repetitive pattern intended to bring something to a close. There is hardly ever anesthesia applied when closing gashes and openings. There is a pain that comes from closure. Another thing to consider is, before holes are closed, they have to be cleaned. God won't bring closure to areas that have not been cleaned from within. He will remove the unclean things that could potentially cause infection and bring further complication. The cleansing process can require additional cutting or digging. Also, as the area experiences regeneration, you will again experience the discomfort of growth or what we know as itching.

For contamination, you will need detoxification. The ingredients of a detox may be hard to swallow already, but as the contamination leaves you, you will experience pains and discomforts that will make you want to quit. If you have ever done any type detox system or natural detox, it could be a very harsh experience. Being able to digest what isn't pleasing is a part of detox. However, the extreme headaches and excessive passing of waste can almost feel unbearable and incomparable to the things you have had to swallow.

We know these treatments are in intended for our good. They are meant to bring us to wholeness, but the process of it all can be excruciating. Your pain tolerance will be pushed.

DECEPTION OF PAIN

Sequential effects give us perspective into all things that need consideration in the complex process of healing. Another sequential effect is addressing the deception of pain. We can be so accustomed to having pain that we don't know how to exist without it. We cling to its existence as if our life depends on it. We sometimes can perceive pain from areas that God has addressed because we are not ready to move forward in the life that is free of pain.

In medicine, there is something called phantom pain. It is a phenomenon that happens to people who have limbs removed. The patient will perceive pain from the limb that is no longer there. It's as if the nervous system is misfiring. The same kind of thing can happen in the soul. We can be so attached to living with pain, when God starts removing it from our hearts, we will still be deceived into holding on to it. It is a false reality and remains until the heart is retrained to love peace. God has to put pressure on the state of mind you are in. This experience can be severely discomforting because you will have to change how you think about and interact with pain.

POSTIONING OF PAIN

Sequential effects also include the transitions that pain produces. When God begins to heal you, it will push you into a new space. We discussed that when talking about sterile environments. We can sometime anticipate the displacement that happens because of the demands of recovery, but what about after? After healing, you may find that you don't fit into the spaces that you used to frequent. Some of those spaces were only attractive and comfortable because they resonated with the broken version of you. You will find that you are in a different shape and need new surroundings. In some instances, this may even be mandatory in order to maintain your healing.

In the eighth chapter of the book of Mark, the scripture records Jesus healing a blind man. It is recorded that Jesus spit on the man's eyes. (This, again, is an application of water as Jesus is the Living Water.) In order to heal the man, Jesus had to lead the man out of the town he was in. As I told you earlier, environments can incubate your brokenness or foster your healing. The healing process was not immediate. Jesus healed his vision (outer sight) and his perception (inner sight).

When the man was completely restored, Jesus told the man to go to his house and not to go to the town nor communicate about his healing to anyone there.

This could potentially be your experience. When you heal, you won't be the same and that may even be in ways that you can't personally see from your point of view. God may sovereignly relocate and reposition you away from people and places that are familiar in order to keep your wholeness. On a deeper note, Jesus did not even attempt to heal him until he led him away. Some of your healing will not start until you go to the outskirts of your normal life and steal away with Jesus. People who know you while broken only see you as your condition. They can and will impact your faith for healing and that's why you must make the move.

ACCEPTANCE

Why are these sequential effects important to know? I tell you this because healing hurts and vulnerability is scary—even when you plan for it. It will be doubly true when you are dealing with God's perfect healing. As much as you want to be fully prepared for everything that will happen, you are just better off yielding to the omniscience of God. We all can be tempted to run for the hills when someone touches areas that we didn't know to authorize or prepare for touching. Go ahead and commit to not quitting. It can feel overwhelming to have the nakedness of your soul exposed. It is in your best interest to just trust God and relax. It can be very hard to confront the way that you think. Don't let your pride and ego get in the way. You don't know as much as you think you do. I want you to go ahead and settle in yourself that nothing is off limits to God. Don't fixate on what you feel needs to be done or how it needs to be done. He knows the way that you should take. He is the one that designed you and understands how to bring you back to wholeness. He knows where you are going and what you need to get there. Accept that in your healing process, you need to relinquish control and surrender to the journey that God has plotted for you. When you let go, that is when you can begin your journey to the river without any hindrances.

Journey Thoughts | Chapter 9

1. How do you come to grips with unavoidable sequential effects of healing?
2. Does the reality of these effects preemptively hinder you or do you simply feel like it's a helpful precaution?
3. Are you self aware enough, at this point, to notice your misdirection of pain?
4. How do you cope with God's response to your emotional hyperaglesia? Does it make you feel negative feelings?
5. How can you mentally prepare for the increased pain that is caused by the healing process?
6. Do you remember a time in the past where you leaned heavily into phantom pain because pain feels like normalcy? As you go on this journey, how will you defend against clinging to phantom pain?
7. What is your response if God instructs you not to return to certain places and relationships in order to stay healed? Do you have the will to do it?
8. Have you processed that this journey will have healthy amounts of pain? Are you prepared to endure it until the end?

Part 4
Strength For Your Journey

JOURNEY TO THE RIVER

Chapter 10 – Testimonies

HEAR THIS

In the previous 8 chapters, I have attempted to share practical wisdom that I believe will help you prepare for and endure your journey ahead. I know that wisdom can seem theoretical because it is normally gained after someone is out of woods on a noteworthy situation of which they may share. I used practical experiences in my life to convey deep wisdom that I learned on my journey to the river. The journey was intense. On some days, I did not want to go any further. Having to come into face-to-face contact with myself was hard. Some of the conversations I had to have were difficult. Sitting in the truth was extremely uncomfortable. In the end, it was work, but it was worth it. Moreover, I was worth it. God interrupted my life in an alarming fashion to get me out of a cycle of mediocrity and brokenness so that I could envision His best for me. However, I'm not the only one with a journey story. I believe that it would do your heart good to hear other people's stories. Testimonies are meant to empower us and encourage our hearts to face whatever is in front of us. They help us overcome. Hearing testimonies from people who were ahead of me (on their journey) was a major boost for me. So, for your encouragement, I've gathered a few stories from brothers and sisters who have had to take their journey to the river. I asked them to share with me: a specific moment or event God used to show them unaddressed pain in their hearts; the journey he took them on to unpack and address the pain; and the benefits of enduring the journey. Some of the journeys were short. Others had to be repeated. Truth is, all of their journeys still happened, were fruitful, and filled with the grace of God. The following passages are their stories in their own words.

TERRANCE'S JOURNEY

Newsbreak: A Local young preacher caught in a Scandal

There was a time that I became conflicted in my inner man concerning my image and reputation, which was not a regular concern for me when I was younger, but because I answered the call to public service, how others perceived me became a great matter of concern. Overtime, I accumulated a number of friends, mentees, and ministry partners that I wanted to impress. I wanted to make sure these people celebrated my messages and were proud of me as their leader. The platforms I developed began to mean more to me than they ever did in the past. I developed a fear of rejection. To be honest, I should say the fear of rejection that was buried underneath, began to unveil.

Everything broke out and my world changed when the areas of immaturity, wickedness, and moral defects became public knowledge. God allowed public shame and attack to remove this fear of rejection. Like Job, the thing that I feared the most had come upon me. Anyone who has ever experienced this knows the kind of shame and embarrassment that accompanies such a tragedy. For many, it is the death of a ministry or a business. In other cases, it is the death of relationships, and in some extreme cases, the shame can lead to a literal death.

The Root Cause of Malpractice

At the root, the moral failure and fear of being exposed was the same thing. Overtime, I recognized that the motivating factors behind my infidelity, promiscuity, and dishonesty were a desperate desire to be liked and praised. Both fear of rejection and pride led to me hiding real internal pain, which caused me to be deceptive.

I have learned that fear can mask itself as vision. I recognize now that many of the things I was doing then was my attempt at trying to drown out the noise of a chaotic heart. I was trying to silence the voices of insecurity. I muted the sounds with busyness in projects and products. I thought that if I just did the good works, I would be accepted as good and I could somehow buy more time to work out the secret wickedness in my soul.

Fear is a powerful force. It caused Pharaoh and Herod to kill masses of Hebrew babies. They feared they would be overthrown and so out of fear of failure and an internal sense of insignificance, they murdered. I learned that my fear made me murderous. When I look back, much of the beginning of my ministry had to do with "calling out" and discrediting successful people in ministry for whatever reason and then trying to build a reputation of "righteousness" off the foundation of exposing people with moral flaws.

I built a team that rejoiced in the exposure and failure of a celebrated figure.

For me, while I was working out inner demons, in religious circles, I was growing in honor and increasing in my giftedness. I moved from being a minister to an elder to being recognized as an apostle and I functioned in that capacity locally and abroad. I thought apostleship would do the same thing I thought marriage would do and I was wrong about both. I thought making a vow and entering into the covenant did something supernaturally to make me different internally. This is why readiness before entering in is critical. I thought that entering into the office would turn me into another man.

Just as getting married doesn't make a person loyal, neither does entering into a heavenly vocation. Becoming an officer of heaven does not magically remove ones proclivities to be hypocritical, lustful, immature, or covetous. It doesn't take away from the calling, but it does take away from the overall purpose of the calling and the purpose for preordination in the first place.

Imagine what it feels like to be going through a divorce and dealing with the death of a loved one at the same time. This is what it is like to go through a scandal. You are divorced from ministry and you experience death to relationships suddenly that you thought you had time to improve upon forever.

Once your reputation has been destroyed, you have the opportunity to rebuild your life in a new way. The worse thing has already happened. Your relationships have already been ruined. You have already been casted as a villain. People's opinions of you have already been formed. You can't go back and fix everything and make it right. You can't brand your intentions or your viewpoints in other people's hearts. Lines have been drawn and sides have been taken. At some point you must choose to pick up the broken pieces and move on with life. This is what happened to me. I lost every relationship that was built on fraudulent grounds. The friendships that were solid endured the most turbulent times. I had to live with not being seen in the way I thought I was. I had to live with knowing that my flaws were public knowledge. I was no longer a local hero. Now I was the conversation piece and the juicy subject of gossip and suspicion. The same thing I did to other preachers was not being done to me. You reap what you sow.

A New Chapter: Lessons Learned

After the tragic events unfolded, I had to go through many emotions such as heartbreak, remorse, anger, pride, etc. But the one that was the most difficult was learning how to forgive my accusers. Overall, I learned so much about the fragility of relationships, reciprocity, and the transformative opportunities that tragedies bring to the human condition. Through the pain I learned how to be more honest with myself, more discerning when choosing friends, more realistic about my ability to manage certain relationships, and more cautious about making choices. My outlook on ministry changed and my message became more understandable and relatable. I became less critical and more merciful, gracious and understanding in my assessment of other people. The experience made me a better minister, but more than that, it made me a better man and for that I am eternally grateful.

NATASHA'S JOURNEY

In the first few years of my marriage I struggled with receiving ANY type of correction, criticism, and even instruction from my husband. I had deep issues with honoring his authority. Conversations would quickly escalate when he would approach me about even the smallest issue. I would reply to him with statements such as "I'm not your child. You won't speak to me any kind of way. I don't know who you think you're talking to...." You know...all of that. I carried on exerting my knowledge, strengths, and (false) power to let it be known that I was not to be handled. My husband was patient, however he would say to me at times, "I am not your father." Which would anger me even more. See the root of the matter was that due to a family history of verbal, emotional, sometimes physical abuse and deep-rooted misogyny; I had strong issues with male authority. I had made up in my mind that no man would ever disrespect or belittle me and it carried over into my marriage. I truly believe that my spouse is anointed to handle my issues—even issues that had nothing to do with him. Issues and hurt that took place before I ever knew him. God used him to call out the source of my pain (I really wasn't even aware of) and help me to heal in an area of abused authority. He used my husband to show me what it meant to submit to one another in love and what balanced healthy authority looks like. Now, I am able to receive teaching, criticism, and instructions from my wonderful man that is helpful, uplifting and loving without being defensive and demanding respect. Our children are able to see a mutually respectful union where we honor one another, where iron sharpens iron, and where we grow together in love.

PATRICK'S JOURNEY

One of the most traumatic years that I have had to endure was 2016. That year highlighted one of the deepest rejections I have had to deal with during my life: rejection from my father. Ever since the announcement I gave about getting married to my fiancé (now wife), it led to one of the biggest altercations I have had with my father but revealed some deep hurt and rejection issues that I have had to grow up with and had the hardest of times overcoming it. That particular year revealed also the things that hindered progression in my life. Every time I would try to move forward, I would always have a major conflict with my father about it. My childhood was filled with moments where no matter how hard I tried to please my father; nothing I did was good enough in his eyes. Whether it was chores, grades, or anything I had a milestone in, it just wasn't enough and ultimately left me feeling rejected. After my heated altercation, that year started a journey of healing, which took some prayer and some faith steps along the way. In my soul, I carried the pain of rejection and feeling undervalued. Although I knew I needed to forgive, my process involved healing in my heart. No matter what kind of pain you endure, I have learned that once you get your heart healed from all the pain of the past, the forgiveness comes as a byproduct. As I continued to pray for my heart to heal and for my father, there were little things that happened in specific moments. One of the moments was when a car that was signed in his name became officially a vehicle titled in my name as well as my wife's. This was a first step in the healing process because up to that point there was no communication. The second thing was when I found out about the prostate cancer diagnosis. My heart began to flood immediately with compassion and prayer for his healing and salvation.

It led me to call my father and pray for him on the spot. At that moment, I knew this is what God wanted me to do and it was in His timing. The biggest breakthrough came through the announcement of telling my parents that they will be grandparents. My Father called me after I spoke with my mom and told me that he was very proud of me. I surprised him with how long I was able to maintain in marriage after he was totally against it. Now my wife and I can come over to my parent's house with no restrictions and no arguments. To this day, I'm still shocked at this but I know the hand of God has been involved with this journey of healing my heart. If there is anything that I want anybody to gain from my testimony, it's that God is a healer of the brokenhearted and he is a reconciler of brokenness within families. Although this journey was rough, it was necessary for God to make all things new.

ASHINNA'S JOURNEY

After adopting my son Jahari, my mom realized I needed some support because this was my first time having a child. Because she was coming, her husband would be coming too. I did not want him to be there, but if it meant having my mother close to me I was willing to tolerate it. The days leading up to him coming, I couldn't sleep. I could not sleep and every night I would wake up. I realized that I had to reconcile this situation before he arrived—before he got to Virginia. God was putting pressure on this unresolved anger. I prayed about it. I went to church and got prayer from leadership at my church. I knew what I had to do I just did not want to do it. I realized that I needed to do it. I knew that the anger I was harboring towards him was holding me back in a lot of ways. God took me on a journey to unpack this anger.

When I was younger, I really disliked my mom's husband for several reasons. It was really hard for me to move past that. When they got married, I think I was 15 years old. My father died when I was 14 and then really swiftly it was like he was just there as my mom's new husband when I turned 15 and I just didn't feel settled with that transition. It happened really fast. I was young and I didn't really know how to process my emotions, and thoughts, and feelings. I think that my default way of dealing with things was to just be silent. So whenever my mom's husband would come around, he would speak to me and say, "Hi Ashinna. How are you doing?" He would ask me how my day was and I would just ignore him. I would just look at him and walk away. I was very angry with him. I felt like everything that was wrong was because of him.

I just had a lot of venom in my veins towards him. I don't remember ever like really hating a person, but in my mind, I just hated him. Everything that I saw happen to my mother from the point where they got married was bad. It was a very sad time for me. I remember crying a lot. I remember emotionally overeating. And that's when I started. Now that I think about it, that's when I started to gain a lot of weight around that time in my childhood. That carried over into my adult life. I think it also carried over into my relationships with men. There were other reasons why I had a lot of fear of trusting men, but that was a big piece of it. This was someone that my mom introduced to my life. At that transitional time when a girl is going from being a little girl to being a big girl, whatever man is around her is supposed to be like a good example. I didn't feel that he was that. I didn't like the way he treated my mom and I didn't even like the way that he was towards me. I remember specifically this one time him telling me, just a year after my father had died, "Yeah! I should have been your father." I just remember going ballistic on him, cursing, and throwing stuff at him.

I was doing things that were completely out of character for me, then and now. At the moment I just hated him. I did.

My mom started using drugs. We became homeless. I didn't know where she was a lot of the time. She just became this other version of herself. That was a sad thing to see. It was sad to watch her deteriorate. She was so little and she just looked like death walking. To be a teenage kid and have to experience that was hard for me. Again, I blamed that on my mother's husband. I know, in my adult mind, that she was an adult making decisions for herself.

In any case, all of this was brought to the surface when they were planning to come. I did not really have the right to judge him or to hold onto my anger towards him because the same forgiveness that God allows for me—he is deserving of it too. I didn't know his entire story. I don't know everything he's been through and I just felt it was not my place. So I called him. I told him how I felt about basically everything and explained to him why and I told him that I forgave him. I told him that I wanted to welcome him and make the move to Virginia a whole brand new start for us. As soon as I did that, immediately, this weight lifted off of me and I just felt really good about myself and I knew that I was honoring God by doing what I was supposed to do. Forgiveness. You're supposed to have it within yourself to forgive people if we follow the model of Christ.

That was a huge turning point and when he did arrive it was a blessing for me to see him interact with Jahari. I think he was the first man that Jahari bonded with. He was the first man that took Jahari outside to make a snowman. He would dress up in silly clothes with him and just do things that made Jahari feel safe. He made him feel validated. It made him feel loved and I don't think that any of that would have happened had I not been obedient and allow myself to release the anger that I had been holding on to since

I was a little girl. I was able to start to talk to him and kind of understand him on it on a different level. And so all of that was definitely a blessing.

Forgiveness is not always easy, but I think, in most instances, you find that it takes a lot more energy for you to keep up the anger, be petty, and be bitter towards a person. A lot of times the person does not care anyway. It really just ends up being a lot of energy that you waste and you could be using it somewhere else.

DARIUS'S JOURNEY

On October 13, 2008, my son was born and I sat in the hospital room with my wife. At the time she wasn't my wife, but she was my son's mother. I remember sitting there hurting. I remember being overwhelmed with separation anxiety because I had broken her heart. There was an issue that was going on within me that brought me to that place. The journey began when God allowed me to experience the pain that I caused the most valuable PERSON IN MY LIFE AT THE TIME NOW AND ALWAYS. Although I had been saved and accepted Christ as Lord, I still needed to grow. I still needed to endure pain so that I could heal properly. In that moment of sobriety, this witnessing the birth of my son and seeing the trauma that I had caused my wife almost destroyed my entire life. I'm so thankful that God saved me and gave me a purpose. He gave me the chance and opportunity to see why I was born. I was born to be used by him to manifest the gift in me—all of the gifts in me, not just one. It was a moment of reckoning. In that time—in that space—sitting in the hospital room, I was watching my wife suffer from PTSD because she had just given birth to my son. She was suffering from PTSD because of the traumatic experience that I had caused her from my fornication, infidelities and inappropriate relationships and not knowing how to take ownership and be a man about my wrongs. I blamed her and I brought more pain and more afflictions on her. I also created my own bondage by not being able to accept, understand, and unpack the issues that were in my heart. They were rooted in separation anxiety, isolation, and alienation.

From the time that I was 7 to 13 I experience so much of that. I moved from Brooklyn New York to Summerton, South Carolina experiencing the death of my brother and other things that were traumatic. Just trauma. When you're 13 and you get your heart broken, it's a traumatic thing because you can't eat. You can't sleep. You can't think. You end up treating women in the ways that you don't want to even talk about. You do all of that to try to hide from the pain. Now, it's somebody you love who's giving birth to your first child and you've done this to them, unbeknownst. And when I say unbeknownst, I don't mean not knowing. I'm not suggesting that I did not know what I was doing, because we always know what we're doing. We always have the choice to make--but, is it the right choice that we're making? Are we choosing wisely? Are we considering the full impact? Most times we aren't. But it was in this time that I was able to understand that there was an issue that I had in my heart and I needed to figure out a way to deal with it. Even though I had accepted the person, Jesus Christ into my life as my lord and savior, I didn't know how to live that out.

So in this moment that my son was born, God was able to stop time for me just to show me what my purpose was and now I have to pursue it. Now I have to go on this journey. Because I didn't know who I was, I have to answer and endure the consequences. I have to endure the consequences for not being in his will and outside of my purpose. I had to unpack over the course of 10 years and discover my identity and purpose.

Now, today I am able to pursue those things. Passionately. If you look back at your life, you can see that there are probably issues and things in your heart that you haven't been able to unpack. Things that just need to surface. Things that just need to come up because they don't need to be in you. It was a moment of clarity for me. Not only does God have to do the work but also you have to do the work with him. In order for you to be who God called you to be, you can't half step it.

It wasn't just all fixed in a moment. Dealing with the trauma of infidelity, it was breaking my heart and breaking me down. I thought that I could avoid the pain but I couldn't control what was going on. Seven or eight years later, after multiple traumatic experiences, I just couldn't find a way to heal my marriage at the time. I ended up being unfaithful. God was breaking me down again. He was taking me into the deepest parts of myself. He was showing me that He was not going to leave me and He was not going to forsake me. There's no greater love than His. There's no pain harsh enough --no pain greater than the love that he has for me. Even though I ended up in the place where I couldn't find hope for healing in my marriage, I was able to find healing for myself and it was really the main thing. It was also the start to a new chapter for my family

Once I was able to understand that my faithfulness was not going to spare me pain, I was able to get clarity and understand my purpose. Today, after all these years and all these traumatic experiences, now I'm able to really and truly pursue healing individually so that I can be truly whole. Being whole isn't just one quick trip to get to. It's a journey. And I'm so excited about the *journey that I have to go on to reach my destiny and purpose. But I've got to say it's a lot of work going on this journey. The resolve for me was understanding that my purpose and understanding that my destiny requires the work of the journey. If you are reading this, I'm praying that you're able to take your journey and be the person that God called you to be because you have to. For you—but more importantly, For Him. For the King of Glory! Peace & Grace!*

TAKE HEED

These brothers and sisters were very transparent. They all wanted to be able to encourage you to take your journey. There were others and they will be shared in other ways. However, experiencing them unravel their journeys in bite size pieces was something to marvel at. The common theme was thankfulness. We live so much life on the road to destiny. Sometimes, life is happening so fast, we rarely have time to pause and reflect in this fashion. My hope is that you will take heed to the wisdom that they shared. I pray that you see the benefit of getting to that river (and understand the potential consequences of not doing so.) Since you've been given wisdom and encouragement, I want stay in the spirit of prayer. As you go into the next chapter, I want to leave you some prayers to help you along your journey to the river. Prayer is paramount! Let us pray!

JOURNEY TO THE RIVER

Chapter 11 — Prayers for the Journey

THE POWER OF PRAYER

You have made it through the preemptive part of your healing journey. You now have the wisdom and insight to prepare you for the work ahead. You now have the encouragement from the testimonies of people who have gone through their journeys. The only thing left for you to do is open up and let yours begin. It's your time to yield to Abba and let him lead you to His waters. I am deeply grateful to Abba on your behalf.

I understand what it's like to experience letting down the walls so I could make it to the healing waters of God. I remember walking the unfamiliar territory. I remember how difficult it was being removed from my comfort zone. I remember feeling awkward because I had to relearn myself. I am *still* learning something new daily. I remember saying things like, "I feel like a raw piece of meat in the hands of butcher" because of the vulnerability and exposure I felt before God. In the end, I know all of it is worth it.

Honestly speaking though, the only thing that regularly helped me stay the course was prayer. I had to consistently stay in communication with God. He was the only one who had a full understanding of what I was experiencing. Not many around me could understand what I was going through. In fact, many of them expected me to be as I always was. They did not know that I was changing and being transformed through healing. My communication with God helped me to yield and trust him even when I felt the most uncertainty, discomfort, and displacement. The healing process completely shifted my daily life and routine. It shifted my company. It shifted my communication style. It shifted my conversations. It was an experience that was being led by God and I had to completely surrender myself to it. That trusting part was hard. This, again is why talking to God is such a necessary part of the journey. You can't just be brought face-to-face with your hidden pains by God and not let him talk you through the process.

So, my admonishment to you is to PRAY without ceasing. I don't mean become religious and feel like you can't do anything but pray. I mean, keep a dialogue going on all day. Notice, I said **DIALOGUE**. Talk and leave intentional space for Him to speak back to your heart. Communicate honestly about how you are feeling and what you are thinking along the way. This ensures that you remain fully present to endure the entire process. Don't be shy in telling God the truth. His responses will often sober you from your pain-drunken perspectives anyway. It will also keep you from quitting. When you are tired, praying will energize you. Regularly find things to tell God thank you for. Going through healing and confronting pain in your heart requires you to process negative times in your life. It is easy to be pulled into a dark space. Prayers of thanksgiving will keep your point-of-view balanced. Prayer will tear down those strongholds that have kept your heart closed off all of these years. Prayer will be the internal GPS that guides you to the water. And along the way, you will find that you have become completely unhindered to heal.

As you end this part of the process, I want to leave you with some prayers to help you start. I don't expect for you to simply read and recite these prayers everyday. Let these prayers be openers for you. Let them serve as accelerants by opening up your heart and spirit through the power of words. After all, I just want to help you apprehend the healing that Abba made a way for you to have. This is your time to be whole. This is your chance to start a new journey. Be brave. You have nothing to lose that is worth keeping and you have everything to gain. My hope and prayer is that you take your Journey to the River and be made whole.

A PRAYER FOR FAITH

Father God, I thank you for loving me so much that you want me to become whole. I thank you for giving your Son, Jesus so that healing could be my right. I thank you for the leading and guidance of your Holy Spirit. I deeply need that guidance today. I thank you for bringing me to this place and allowing me to have survived in spite of all of the challenges that I have faced. I thank you for your mercy and patience that has covered me while I was not my best self in life, positions, relationships, or any of those things. I thank you for today being a new day with new opportunities to become the person that you have designed me to be. I honor you and give you glory for that. I know I have a lot of hurdles to climb to get to wholeness but I am asking for the faith to go beyond what I can see. I pray that you will give me the ability to believe your plan for my life. I ask to have my faith increased to see a new beginning for me. I ask that you increase my capacity to envision my life becoming different from the inside out. Let my faith be stronger than my fears when this journey gets complicated. Let my faith in you pull me through to your healing waters when I would rather quit. Let my doubts be drowned out and overcome by faith. Let all of the negative words that have been spoken over me be muted in my soul while your truths echo loudly. Let those truths form a picture in my heart that I might look toward on my journey. Let me be fueled by faith in your goodness. Let me remember your goodness as I am being made new. I know this process will hurt and cost me, but I know it is for my good. Let faith embolden me and thrust me toward hope in a future that you have already fully planned for me. Let me be reminded that you are God with me now and you are God of my future. Let the faith for healing and wholeness arise in me now!

IN JESUS NAME, AMEN!

A PRAYER FOR TRUTH & HONESTY

Father, I love you and I thank you for your SPIRIT OF TRUTH that is with me. When everything around me is a lie, GOD you are true. I thank you for Jesus Christ, my savior who is the way, the truth, and the life. I thank you for being the God of truth. I thank you for being able to stand behind your words because you are TRUE. I thank you for being faithful over your words. I thank you that truth prevails in you. Because you are true, I can trust you. I am thankful that I can trust you. I trust you to give me truth even when it may be uncomfortable to me. Because you are true, Father, you are my safe place. There is no shadow of turning in you. Your integrity is unmatched and for that I am grateful. I pray now, Father, that your HOLY SPIRIT will now lead me and guide me into all truth—TRUTH about my history and pain. I pray to be confronted with the truth about myself. Allow me, God, to be able to see what is hidden within me. Allow my eyes to see it all plainly. Let me truthfully discern what is in my heart, Father. Let no pride or deception cause me to be blinded by lies. I pray to be able to see myself as I am and as you have called me to be. I know that I cannot heal from what is not revealed. Give me the boldness to stand in the truth. Let me have the integrity to be honest about my brokenness. Father, allow me to see my holes. Expose, in me, the lies that are embedded in my heart. Let me be honest with myself about my pain. Let every falsehood that I have adopted in my personality be destroyed by your word of truth. Let the belt of Truth uphold me as my broken frame is made whole again. Lord, I pray for the strength to face the truth.

IN JESUS NAME, AMEN.

A PRAYER FOR COURAGE

God, I thank you for being a good Father. I know that you are with me and you cover me. Your presence gives me security. I thank you for the strength of your presence. I thank you for my LORD and savior, Jesus Christ, who is the man of flawless victory. He has never faced any opponent and lost. He has never had one of his own slip from his hands. Because He is with me, I have the boldness to move toward the hard fights. I pray now for Godly courage to do things outside of my comfort zone. I pray that you empower me to face truth and do things in faith. Lord I need courage to have difficult conversations in spite of fear. Father I need courage to rise up in me to take strides toward my healing even in the midst of doubting so that I can be whole. Help me, father, to be strong and of great courage. Give me the holy boldness to break family cycles, end toxic relationship, and move out of unproductive environments. Give me the courage to tell the truth even when there has been generational suppression of the truth in my family or household. Give me the courage break free from iniquitous patterns in my bloodline. Give me the courage to resist social norms that are under demonic influence—in spite of feeling ousted from my peers. Give me the courage to face my true self and abandoned the representative that I created in my efforts to cope with trauma. Give me the courage to do the hard work of unpacking my pain with you, God. Give me the courage to follow you to a new place that I have never been. Let your courageousness empower me now O' LORD.

IN JESUS NAME, AMEN.

A PRAYER FOR PATIENCE

Father, I thank you for being a GOD who has and continues to be patient with your people. Your ability to suffer long was proven time and time again throughout scripture. YOUR greatest display of patience is given in your son, JESUS CHRIST. I thank you JESUS for what you endured on the cross on my behalf. In spite of how hard it was for you, you called it 'the joy set before [you]'. I thank you for demonstrating the ability to endure to the end of a thing. I know that because I have your spirit, I can also patiently endure to the end even when it is hard. Father, I pray that you would cause your patience to spring forth in me during this process. Like my Lord Jesus, let me have the results of this healing in view. Allow me to see its impact as a place of joy that I am endeavoring to apprehend. Let me remember the generational impact that my healing will have. Father, help me to envision the lives of those you have called me to during this healing process. Let this sober me when the pain is intense and seemingly unyielding. Help me to stay in the place, position, and posture that you ask of me throughout this process. Help me to not rush your work and stay connected to your timing. Father, help me to not skip over parts of the process but endure each step until it all is complete. Your word says "Let patience have her perfect work, that we may be made perfect and complete, lacking in nothing" I pray that patience begins her perfect work in me right now so that I can be made whole.

IN JESUS NAME, AMEN.

A PRAYER FOR FOCUS

My Father and God, I thank you for directing the lives of your children. I thank you specifically for directing me. I thank you for your wisdom and correction. I thank you for your staff and your rod because they comfort me. I thank you for your voice that calls out to me to lead me to the healing waters. I pray now, father, that you help me to focus my heart on this journey that you are calling me on. As shepherds do, I pray that you will pull me in when I attempt to wander off. I pray that your voice would locate me when I am distracted by what appears to be an easier fix. Help me to intensify my self-control. Give me the strength to deny my flesh in discipline. Help me to increase my ability to focus on what you have set before me. Your scripture says that your sheep hear your voice and another they will not follow. Father, sound mark my life so that I am not drawn away by various voices that would prematurely set me in places, positions, or postures. Let me not be distracted by anyone else's process or timeline. Keep my heart aligned with your plan and strategy. Let me not sabotage your work by inserting myself in ways that aren't necessary. I pray for the consistent ability to give myself completely to this process. Let my focus increase now,

IN JESUS NAME, AMEN.

A PRAYER FOR SUPPORT & SURROUNDINGS

Thank you father for surrounding me with your presence and comfort. Thank you for upholding me by the strength of your right hand. Thank you for being my shield and buckler. Thank you for covering me under the feather of your wings and hiding me in your shadow ALMIGHTY GOD. Thank you for hovering over me just as mother hen hovers over her baby chicks. Thank you for surrounding me with a peace that passes all of my ability to understand. I pray now, father, that you would purify my environment. Help me to separate myself from people, places, and things that will not be helpful on my healing journey. Let the words of my mouth and the meditations of my heart please you and echo your declarations as it pertains to my destiny. Lord, I pray that you crowd my life with the people you have appointed to be on this journey with me. Let me be aware of the voices that are anointed for my life in this season. I pray to be courageous enough to create distance in those relationships that are toxic or contributors to my current state. Holy Spirit, lead me, as only you can, to the right places and right people each day. Let my discernment be open so that I may be aware of what is happening around me. I thank you now Father for the safety that comes from the multitude of counselors. I pray that those you staff my life with, have mouths filled with your wisdom and hearts tempered by your mercy and truth. Crowd my life with your words and your ways now.

IN JESUS NAME, AMEN.

ALWAYS PRAY

Pray without ceasing. Be in continual communion with Abba. When you feel like quitting: *pray*. When you feel empty: *pray*. When you feel all of your hurt at the surface: *pray*. When you feel overcome with emotion: *pray still*. Our Heavenly Father is not fragile or taken aback by our experiences in reality. In addition to whatever other healthy things you do to address your pain and emotional brokenness, always include prayer. Keep it at the top of the list. Maintaining your connection to heaven will be your sustaining power. As I said before, Abba will sober your heart as you include Him. Make your first step to your journey in prayer.

JOURNEY TO THE RIVER

Chapter 12 – Final Words of Wisdom

YOUR JOURNEY BEGINS NOW

Beautiful Soul! I started off greeting you and now I want to bid you farewell. I say farewell because I know that when Abba finally gets you to that river, He will make you completely new just as He did for Naaman. Even more personally, just like He did for me. Your amazing journey is present before you here and now. Either you are preparing to take your first steps or you are preparing to put your feet back on the path. God is calling you to the river no matter the position you currently find yourself. Yes, there is tremendous work to be done. There is so much to have to deal with. But having said that, I still know, without a doubt, that this is the most amazing journey you will take.

Throughout this book, I have attempted to encourage and prepare you for the journey that awaits you. I have attempted to precaution you for some of the resistance that you may face along the way. It is my hope to have given you a glimpse into your potential outcomes in various phases in the journey. On your road to destiny, there is a river that always runs parallel to its path. No matter the terrain of life, you will always have a path that cuts to a river. Because there is no route to destiny that allows us to avoid the tolls of pain, the bridges of disappointment, or the traffic of trauma, we will always need to pull over and take a journey to the river. The beautiful thing is that if you yield to God, he will lead you to your river, as often as you need refreshing and healing.

The river experience will be different for each of us. In fact, each circumstance or season may require a different river location. Metaphorically, the river is the environment that has been appointed to host the healing presence of God specifically for you. Some river locations will be beautiful and smooth. Some will be ferocious and dirty. The power isn't really in the river itself. It is but a conduit of the GRACE of GOD. Your submission to His leadership and your commitment to His instructions will grant you the outcome that you are after. On a deeper revelatory note, the river is Christ, the ANOINTED ONE. The invitation for a journey to the river is always and invitation to come into the intimate proximity of Christ. The goal is to be immersed in the presence of His Spirit. He is the spirit of truth and the spirit of counsel & might. All wisdom and healing flow from his mind and power. He is the safe refuge and repairer of the broken. He is the one that lifts heaviness from you and gives new garments so that you are cloth in your right mind. He is the restorer of joy and the lifter of your head. He is the prince of peace. He is the chief strategist for your healing plan. He knows who to assemble in your supporting cast. Coming into close proximity with Him is worship and intimacy. Intimacy breaks you open. Worship transforms you. Christ is truly the Great Physician and He mends the broken hearted. All in all, He is your great river.

There are forces and circumstances from within and around you that will try to impede you on your journey to the great river. Thorns, beasts, and serpents may try to intercept your path. You may run into the mental and emotional lions, tigers, and bears while you move to healing. You cannot let any of that keep you from your wholeness. The objective is to get to the river to be restored to wholeness and then resume the trip on the road to destiny. The river is never the final place. You may sojourn there a while but there is an appointed time where the healing work will be complete and you will be ready to go.

One of the most awesome things I like about the river is the current and flow of its streams. Rivers are not stagnant waters. They have movement. This is important because when in healing you are not held back. You can still be moving forward even *off road*. The grace of God has the power to allow you to remain in sync with heaven in spite of the derailment of pain and trauma. You don't have to lose time because it can be redeemed. You may also find that your time in the river accelerates you in destiny. You may come out of the water and be translated to a whole new place in God's story written about you. This is a magnificent part about being in relationship with the sovereign Almighty.

WISDOM SPEAKS

To summarize the collective wisdom: before you set out on the journey throw away your clocks and timelines. Healing is not choreographed like a synchronized swim that you do with a group. It is personal and unique. Avoid self-medicating and if you have already been doing that, set down the alternatives. To quote a song lyric, "Ain't nothing like the real thing, baby." Allow the symptoms and things that spring out of your heart to convey the truth about where you are. It is only in that vulnerability and fearlessness that you have the audacity to own your pain. Don't let anyone silence you and keep you bound to the hidden torture that pain is causing you. Don't even succumb to the fear that may emerge from the depths. Be brave and experience the power of full disclosure. Allow Abba to staff your life and follow his leading so that you can maintain a sterile healing environment every step of the way. Don't get in a rush or forgo steps in the process because you can heal wrong. I know for sure you don't want to complicate the journey. Once you hit the refreshing waters of the river, be postured for the sequential effects. Healing is a beautifully intricate process and you are worth all of it. Jesus definitely thinks so.

To leave you with one final nugget of wisdom: Allow your heart to trust God. Sometimes the real challenge in the journey isn't the pain or the secondary pain that the healing process may create. It is the fear of the unknown. It is the letting go of the reins and not having control of the process. It is the fear of having to meet the new version of yourself—the whole version. You've mastered life as the broken version of yourself and having to learn yourself without the fractures of trauma and pain can be such a weird place. For so long your personality was constructed by fragments, fractures and voids. As you heal, your soul will begin to reintegrate and acclimate to its original state. My admonishment to you is to keep your eyes toward God and lean into him with your whole heart. As you behold him, you will learn of Him and He will teach you about the person he designed you to be even before planet earth had form. His wisdom and love will crowd your life in the unsuspecting ways. All you have to do is extend your trust. In fact, your trust level may not start at 100%. As you lean in, you will find that He is a strong tower and He is a safe place for you. He won't drop you or let you drown in your river journey. You will visit the dark places of your history to reclaim the parts of you that were meant to be with you on the road to destiny. Do not withdraw. To quote David's 139th Psalm, "'Oh he even sees me in the dark! At night I'm immersed in the light!' It's a fact: darkness isn't dark to you…" There is no low place that He won't bend toward to pull you into wholeness. Yield with great fervor and allow yourself to be immersed all the way under the currents of His love until you, like Naaman, are completely restored.

SEE YOU LATER

All of my sayings have come to an end. It's on you to bravely take your journey to the river. I'm praying for you and heaven is cheering you on. I may not be there physically as you walk your path to the water, but take the wisdom with you. I won't completely say goodbye, but, I will say see you later. I await you on the road to destiny. After all, that's what the journey is for.

www.ingramcontent.com/pod-product-compliance
Lightning Source LLC
Chambersburg PA
CBHW070452100426
42743CB00010B/1593